I DIDN'T BELIEVE IT EITHER

One Dad's Discovery
That Everything Is Better Without Alcohol

Todd Kinney

Leaning Rock Press

Leaning Rock Press,
Gales Ferry, CT 06335
leaningrockpress@gmail.com
www.leaningrockpress.com

978-1-960596-18, Hardcover
978-1-960596-19-2, Softcover
978-1-960596-20-8, eBook

Library of Congress Control Number: 2023920223

Cover design byAnnika Wooton

Publisher's Cataloging-in-Publication Data
(Prepared by Cassidy Cataloguing's PCIP Service)

Names:	Kinney, Todd, 1975- author.
Title:	I Didn't Believe It Either : One Dad's Discovery That Everything Is Better Without Alcohol / Todd Kinney.
Other titles:	I Did Not Believe It Either
Description:	Gales Ferry, CT : Leaning Rock Press, [2023] | Includes bibliographical references.
Identifiers:	ISBN: 978-1-960596-18-5 (hardcover) | 978-1-960596-19-2 (softcover) | 978-1-960596-20-8 (ebook) | LCCN: 2023920223
Subjects:	LCSH: Recovering alcoholics. | Alcoholics--Family relationships. | Fathers. | Alcoholism-- Psychological aspects. | Alcoholics--Rehabilitation. | Drinking of alcoholic beverages--Social aspects. | LCGFT: Self-help publications. | BISAC: SELF-HELP / Substance Abuse & Addictions / Alcohol.
Classification:	LCC: HV5275 .K56 2023 | DDC: 362.292--dc23

Printed in the United States of America

For my family

Contents

CHAPTER ONE

Checking the Tires

From the moment I opened my eyes that morning, I knew I was going to puke at some point that day—I just didn't know when. My mouth was pasty and dry, my head throbbed every time I blinked, and my stomach felt like even the slightest smell could induce dry heaves. I felt like death.

It was the winter of 2010 and we were living in my parents' basement. My wife, Beth, and I were building a house and had sold our previous one, so we needed a place to live for (we thought) six months, but it turned out to be nine months. We had three boys at the time, all under the age of six. My parents—in a move they probably still regret to this day—graciously offered up their house. Luckily, they still lived in the big house that my siblings and I grew up in. The basement had three bedrooms, two bathrooms, and plenty of living space. But if you ever want to really discover how destructive little boys can be, move into someone else's house.

Beth and I had gone out the night before—nothing spectacular, just a night out with friends at dinner and then a bar afterward. More than enough time to get shitfaced, though. As I lay in bed dreading the inevitable puking episode, I tried to piece together the latter stages of the night. I remembered dinner, and I remembered the first hour or so at the bar. After that, things got sketchy. I remembered bits and pieces of

1

conversations, but just moments in time. I didn't remember getting home. Beth drove, right? She had to have driven. I had no idea how drunk she was, but surely she wouldn't have let me drive home. Was she mad at me? Did I make an ass of myself? Did I say or do anything stupid? Did we have to leave early because I got too drunk? Did my wallet and cell phone make it home? The all-too-familiar self-interrogation took place inside my head.

Little boys under the age of six are loud and don't like to sleep late, so Beth and I tried to get them out of the house on weekend mornings whenever we could. This particular Saturday morning was no exception; they were all up by 7 am. I took them to get donuts. I was the one who took them, instead of Beth, as an unspoken but mutually agreed-upon punishment for getting too wasted the night before, and because the night before couldn't have been *quite that bad* if I got up early and took my kids for donuts, like a good dad does.

So, off we went to the donut shop. The boys were bouncing around like we were headed to Disney, without a care in the world. I was just trying to put one foot in front of the other and avoid any sudden movements because my head felt like a construction zone. The boys were oblivious that I was living one minute at a time. Today was going to be all about survival.

We arrived at the donut shop and the boys ordered donuts. I did not, even though I love donuts. I knew better than to try to eat anything at that point. We sat in one of those classic donut-shop booths with hard plastic benches and a white table in the middle. I sat in the corner of the booth, trying to calm the construction zone by resting my head where the back of the booth met the wall. When that didn't work, I sat with my elbows on the table and my head resting on both my hands. I rubbed my hands over my eyes, then around my temples, which brought momentary relief but not much else. I would've given anything to be back in bed at that moment. The boys talked. And talked and talked some more. I nodded when it felt like I should nod. I said "Oh, really?" when it felt like I should say that. I said "That's interesting" when it felt like they'd said something they thought would be interesting. I heard them, but I wasn't processing their words—that was too much work. I may have still been legally drunk.

We got back into the car and I started dreaming of the possibility of going back to sleep when I got home, now that I had done my good-dad duty, which clearly mitigated my drunkenness just eight hours prior. My dream was interrupted abruptly, first by the feeling of saliva building up in my mouth, next by my stomach starting to turn and jump, then by my throat lurching. Shit! I needed to pull over!

I quickly scanned my options and decided on the parking lot of a Chinese restaurant about six blocks away. I sped up, took a sudden left into the parking lot, and pulled the car into a spot that wasn't even a designated parking spot. I threw the transmission into park about the same time I opened my door, got out, crouched down by the driver's-side wheel—where I was hoping none of the boys could see me—and threw up three times. The last time was almost all dry heave, which ended with me coughing loudly and forcefully while the veins on the side of my head throbbed. Blood rushed to my head, which was a mere foot from the cold pavement. "I hope the radio is loud enough that the boys can't hear me," I thought. I also remember thinking that I was glad I hadn't parked on a hill, so the vomit couldn't roll back toward my shoes.

I stood up and let the cold morning air hit me in the face, hoping it would help steady me. Then I hurried back into the car, convinced that someone I knew was going to drive by, stop, and ask what I was doing in the parking lot of a closed Chinese restaurant at 9:00 in the morning on a Saturday. I plopped into the driver's seat, queasy and lightheaded. The sun shone through the windshield like a spotlight, onto my hand and the beads of sweat that dotted my skin. I took a deep breath. The blood drained from my head. I looked into the rear-view mirror, where I could see the eyes of two of my boys. Looking at their innocent faces, blissfully unaware of what had just happened, jolted me.

My oldest son asked me why we'd pulled over. "I had to check the tires," I told him.

What the fuck was I doing? Here I was, a grown-ass adult with three kids in the back seat. I was living in my parents' basement, pulled over in an empty Chinese food restaurant parking lot on a Saturday morning (not on a hill, at least!). And I was hung over, throwing up on the pavement while my kids waited in the back seat of my car. Is this what I wanted out of life? Is this what I wanted for my kids? Is this the kind of dad I wanted to be? Wasn't it time to grow up? I hated how this felt.

I got drunk the next weekend.

CHAPTER TWO

Family Ties

I had, by all accounts, an unremarkable childhood. I don't mean that it was boring or nondescript. I mean that it was void of any of the sort of major traumas that often form the root of someone's drinking issues. My parents did not divorce. Nobody super close to me died. I was not molested. I did not grow up in an abusive household. Those are all things I used to associate with drinking problems. People who dealt with that kind of stuff were the ones who had drinking problems, right? *They* were the ones who grew up to be alcoholics.

I actually lived a blessed life growing up. It was a very typical upper-middle-class home life. I always felt very fortunate to grow up with the parents I did. They gave my siblings and me a very stable and safe upbringing. We didn't lack for any of life's essentials (even if we thought we did). I grew up with just about every benefit a person could hope for: attentive, loving, and supportive parents, a nice house, food on the table, and economic security.

With all the advantages this afforded me, it also subconsciously served as a barrier to recognizing my own issues with alcohol later in life. We tell ourselves a lot of lies before we come to grips with our drinking. One of my lies was that, because I had such a "normal" childhood, I could not possibly be an alcoholic or have issues with alcohol. After all, there was nothing from my childhood that would have set me down that path. I just liked to drink, that's all. How could I have a problem when I didn't have any of those issues that lead to drinking problems? Plus, my dad drank every night and he was fine. See? I was fine too.

With addiction, though, there doesn't have to be some big trauma. Alcohol by itself is very addictive—one of the most addictive drugs on earth. The very makeup of alcohol is designed to make you dependent on it. It can cause physical changes in the brain's chemistry. Plus, I have addictive and obsessive tendencies anyway. When you throw an already addictive substance on top of that, of course it's going to cause problems. Just because there's no triggering trauma doesn't mean you're immune from alcohol issues.

I am the oldest of four kids. My dad is a lawyer. My mom was a teacher who stopped working to take care of us kids, then eventually went back to work as an administrator at an assisted-living facility. My mom is everything a mom is supposed to be: supportive, compassionate, and understanding. She always knew the right thing to say or do, no matter what the situation. As a parent myself, I know this isn't always the case (or never!), but my mom sure did fake it well. Because of her, I knew I was loved unconditionally. She also drilled into me to always trust my gut—something I'm thankful for on an almost-daily basis (more on this later).

Shortly after I turned sixteen, I rear-ended someone. It was a very minor accident, but for a newly minted driver it was pretty traumatic. I knew I'd screwed up. I was worried about how much it was going to cost to fix the other car. I was worried about getting in trouble. I came home crying. My mom met me in the entryway, gave me that look that only your mom can give you, and hugged me. She didn't say anything. She didn't ask what happened. She didn't yell at me. She just hugged me. I hugged her back and cried some more. I still remember how that hug calmed me. I remembered that hug the first time one of my kids had a similar accident.

My dad was a dad through and through. I looked up to him and wanted to be like him. I would spend hours in his closet, putting together suit-and-tie combinations that, if I were a real-life lawyer, I would wear to the office. I would bring the pants, then the shirt, then the coat and the tie out to the bed until I found the perfect combination. My dad taught me how important it was to be honest and how a reputation takes a long time to build but is only one bad decision away from falling apart. Whenever we discussed current events or something that had happened to someone we knew, he often responded by saying, "Put yourself in their shoes and think about what it must be like for them." I've carried that with me. I find myself doing that with my own kids all the time, and my dad is why.

In our house growing up, like in a lot of homes, alcohol was just part of everyday life. It was there when company came over. It was there when no company came over. It was there at parties and celebrations. It was there at family gatherings. It was there at meals. It was there during good times. It was there during sad times. It was just there, all the time, like the kitchen sink and the wallpaper. In contrast, my wife grew up in a household where alcohol was much more outwardly toxic, where there were external consequences. Alcohol was something that was abused and something that led to bad things happening. When she first met my family and started hanging out at family events, she remarked at how nice it was that our family treated alcohol in a different manner—something that was just a fun part of social events. It was refreshing for her to see alcohol being consumed without the accompanying consequences she had grown up with. On the surface, it seemed so much more normal.

For much of my life, I certainly thought it was normal. Every single night growing up, my dad had three Seagrams & sodas, each one a little heavier on the Seagrams than the last.[*] And he usually drank even more on the weekends. I'm guessing he caught a decent buzz most nights. When he traveled, he packed a plastic bottle filled with his Seagrams. Not the little, airplane-size bottle—I'm talking the 750 ml-size bottle. I didn't think much about any of this at the time, partly because there didn't seem to be any external consequences for his drinking. He didn't abuse my mom. There wasn't yelling and screaming. There weren't police visits, job losses, or any of the things people associate with "normal" drinking issues. My dad worked hard. He was (and is) a very well-respected lawyer. He was successful. He's a great dad who was always there for me. He was at the

---

[*] There was one exception: the night before my dad had a colonoscopy, he wasn't allowed to drink. I remember him choking down the watery orange liquid that chained you to the bathroom for hours. I remember that night more because he didn't drink than because of the colonoscopy.

games and the school functions. He showed up. I've always had a great relationship with him. For much of my life, I took all that to mean that drinking too much was okay as long as you kept your shit together.

My mom drinks, but hardly ever more than one glass. I remember my dad telling me when I was around 25 years old that, in all the time he'd known my mom, he'd never seen her drunk. I found this to be astonishing—borderline impossible. That was like telling me that "in all the years I've known your mom, I've never seen her eat food."

I was twelve years old the first time I remember seeing my dad drunk. My parents had gone out with some friends, and I babysat the friends' kids. When they all came home, only my mom came into the house to get me. I walked out to the driveway where my parents' car was running. I was surprised to see my dad sitting in the passenger seat. Usually when my parents were together, my dad drove. I opened the door and crawled into the back seat. The radio was unusually loud. My mom turned it down. My dad didn't say anything. He had a wry smile on his face that made him look like he didn't have a care in the world. He thumped his fingers on the window frame to the beat of the music.

After we pulled into the garage and were walking into the house, my mom fumbled with the door handle leading into the house. My dad was behind her, a step below. I was standing behind both of them, on the garage floor. My dad turned around and stared at me with a combination of bewilderment and amusement that I'd never seen before. It was like he couldn't believe my mom couldn't get the door open and found it hysterical at the same time. It was such a strange look. I didn't know how to respond. I just looked away, pretending I hadn't seen him. I wasn't quite sure what was going on. I just knew things were weird and I didn't like it. I was uncomfortable.

My mom got the door open and I hurried upstairs to the safety of my room. A few minutes later, I heard my mom ask my dad whether he was okay. I walked to the hallway and peered down into the section of the entryway that was visible from above. I saw my dad hunched over, with his right arm on the railing and his head resting on his arm—like someone who felt he was going to faint. I felt even more unsettled and uncomfortable than before. What was he doing? Was he sick? I had no idea. I was simultaneously worried about my dad and also just wanted to go to bed and forget it all, which is what I did. When I saw him the next morning, he seemed fine.

"Maybe last night was nothing. Maybe I overreacted," I thought. It was a relief to think that was all it had been.

Around this same time, my uncle entered treatment for alcohol abuse. I remember writing him a letter while he was at his treatment center and going to visit him in what I think was some sort of halfway house. I suppose I had whatever understanding of addiction/treatment at the time that any twelve-year-old kid would have. Shortly after my uncle finished treatment, he and his family were at our house. I don't remember whether we all went out or just the adults did, but my uncle's sobriety must have been on my mind because I remember my dad drinking that night. He didn't get super drunk, but he had enough to drink that I noticed.

We were all gathered in the family room, sitting around talking. My dad was sitting on the floor with his back against the built-in cabinets, throwing a nerf football up in the air to himself over and over. He would chime in with comments that just didn't "fit" with the rest of the conversation. It wasn't really the comments per se, it was the fact that everyone else in the room was sober and he wasn't. When you're having a normal conversation and everyone in the room is sober except one person, the drunk guy tends to stand out.

So often, my dad was the only drunk person in the room. I was so perplexed that my dad would get drunk in front of his brother who recently had been through treatment to quit drinking. I just assumed everyone would abstain from drinking around him, so as to not trigger a relapse. Mind you, I have no idea what my uncle's sobriety was like at that point, nor do I know whether it even bothered him. It's just one of the times I remember my dad's drinking as being something that didn't seem normal.

The memory of my dad's drinking that sits with me the most occurred the night before I left for college. I was heading off to the University of Iowa; my best friend since age five happened to be heading to Grinnell College, which was about 50 miles west of Iowa City. My family and my friend's family ended up spending our last night before college at a hotel close to both colleges. That night, my dad drank. Again, nothing extraordinary happened, but I remember thinking, "Really, you're going to get drunk tonight? Of all nights, the night before I leave for college? Do you have to do it on my last night?" We didn't get into a fight about it. I didn't say anything about it. In fact, I don't remember this being all that traumatic at the time. I don't remember having any lingering sadness, or bitterness, or anything like that. But it must have impacted me on some level, because I still remember it today.

Thirty years later, I easily can imagine the kind of drinking that was going on that night—because I did it myself all the time. It was the kind where I'd have more to drink than everyone else. I wouldn't get fall-over drunk, but most likely I'd be the only drunk person in the room. While everyone else would have a drink with dinner and maybe one or two more before calling it quits, I'd keep going. I did this because I loved drinking, and it was hard to stop when everyone else did. In fact, the very idea of stopping was foreign. "Stop . . . after two drinks? Why? I'm not even drunk yet. That doesn't make sense. Let me get a buzz going, and then I'll think about stopping." (Even though the buzz often inhibited thoughts of stopping). Next thing you know, I'd have had five drinks to everyone else's two, I'd be drunk when nobody else was, everyone knew it but didn't really say anything, and I'd wake up the next morning wondering why it was necessary to drink so much more than everyone else. I did this all the time.

CHAPTER THREE

Late Bloomer

I did a lot of dumb stuff in high school, although my biggest downfall was simply getting caught for just about all of it. If I gave you a list of everything I got in trouble for while growing up, you might think I was a habitual criminal. I promise you I wasn't—it's just that I got caught for 97% of the bad stuff I did.

During my sophomore year of high school, a friend of mine named Mike discovered that our English teacher's file cabinet was not secured with a lock. He further discovered that the very same file cabinet contained every test we would be given throughout the semester. Mike was never one to let an opportunity pass him by. During lunch one day, when our English teacher's classroom, as well as the ones around it, were empty, Mike snuck away and helped himself to the tests in the file cabinet. He then passed them out to anyone who was interested. I was among the interested.

Not being the criminal masterminds we thought we were, a group of us brought copies of the stolen test to my house and studied together the night before the exam. The next day, we all did remarkably well on the exam, and were pretty satisfied with ourselves. The perfect crime, right?

My parents were hardly ever in my car. So, of course, the day after the test my mom happened to drive my car for some reason. This would not have been a problem—except that I had left a copy of the stolen test in the back seat of my car.

"What's this?" she asked, holding the stolen test in her hand when I saw her later that day.

Blood drained from my head. "Holy shit, how does she have that?!?" I thought to myself, forgetting that I had stupidly left the test in my car. "Think of something! Anything!" I tried to look and sound calm.

"That's an old test that Ms. Hargus gave us to use as a study guide."

Now that's some quick thinking. Nice work! I was patting myself on the back.

Even better, my mom seemed satisfied with my explanation. "Oh, okay," was all she said.

It turned out that she was not quite as satisfied with my explanation as I'd thought. My mom, the former teacher, was tutoring students from my school who were homebound for extended periods. That job required her to meet regularly with teachers at the school to discuss the students' assignments and their progress while they were out of school. One of the teachers she met with just happened to be my English teacher. My mom asked her whether she'd given her students an old test to use as a study guide.

Now, at this point, the English teacher still was not aware of what we'd done. My mom didn't disclose all that at the time. But she now had a decision to make: turn her son in or let it slide.

The next day, I was called down to the office. The test-stealing scheme wasn't even on my mind, and I was blissfully unaware of what awaited me. I was escorted to a conference room, where I saw the vice principal, my English teacher, and my mom sitting at the table. Uh oh. Suddenly, the conference room turned into an interrogation room with cement walls and a single light bulb hanging from the ceiling. I wanted to turn around and run. I wanted to cry. Thankfully for me, I was not confronted with the dilemma of snitching on the rest of my friends. Because they had been at my house the night before the test, their involvement was already known. I admitted to everything. There was no use in trying to lie my way out of it. We were caught red handed, and I am one of the world's worst liars anyway.

Mr. Van Wort, the vice principal, then called Mike down to the conference room. Unlike me, Mike was a good liar. Part of me admired how good he was at it. I was always in awe of how he could lie so easily and convincingly. For me, lying took a lot of work, and I was very unsure of myself when I did it. For Mike, it came effortlessly and looked so easy. It was like a superpower.

It seemed like about two hours of tense silence went by while we waited for Mike to make his way down to the office. I spent most of that time alternating between wondering whether I would see daylight for the rest of that quarter and whether Mike would have the balls to lie when he got into the room. Surely he wouldn't. Surely he would see us sitting there and know the gig was up, right?

Mike came in hot. He was ready to poker-face this thing to the death if necessary.

"I don't know what you're talking about," he said to the vice principal.

I was dying inside. "Don't do this!" I was screaming to myself—trying to communicate by glaring at him that they knew everything. "Why are you doing this?!" I yelled inside. I was sweating for him.

The vice principal sat there in a mix of exasperation, annoyance, and rage. I'm guessing he was thinking something along the lines of, "Really? This little fucker is going to try to lie his way out of this? Are you kidding me?!"

I don't think he even said anything to Mike in response. He just sat there. He let the silence do the speaking. It worked. Eventually, Mike sort of accepted what was happening. But he still wasn't ready for a mea culpa. He—somewhat heroically?—wanted to save his partners in crime.

"Mr. Van Wort, let's make a deal," he said.

Oh, Jesus. This should be good.

"I'll take the heat for everyone."

The vice principal was not impressed with Mike's valor.

"YOU'RE IN NO POSITION TO BE MAKING A DEAL!" he shouted as he pounded his fist on the table and rose up from his chair. It felt like he was close to lunging across the table to strangle Mike at any minute. I'm sure he wanted to.

That pretty much ended the meeting. Mike received a couple days of out-of-school suspension. Along with the others who had come over to my house the night before the test, I received a couple of days of in-school suspension. We received an F on the test in question. I had to work my ass off the rest of the semester just to salvage a C in the course.

After I served my suspension and was back in class, I remember another teacher telling me that she really admired what my mom had done, that she didn't know whether she would be able to do the same thing, and that one day I would be thankful she'd turned me in. I was skeptical. Of course, at the time, I didn't fully appreciate or understand everything my teacher was saying. I had very little concept of how difficult a decision it must have been for my mom. I put myself in her shoes now and realize it would be excruciating to have to do that. (Warning to my kids: As hard as it would be, I WOULD do it!)

***

About a year later, our family had returned home from an Easter weekend trip out of town. We didn't have school the next day, so my friends and I were going to hang out that night. For some reason, I asked my sister to come along. My mom told me later that she felt so good that my sister and I were doing something together. We were ten and a half months apart but went to different schools. We didn't run in the same crowd as teenagers. My mom's warm feeling did not last long.

In the neighborhood where one of my friends lived there was a man that my friends liked to torment. They would drive by his house several times a night, yell stuff out the window, honk the horn, and generally act like rude jackasses. They did this for no particular reason, other than that it always got a reaction out of him. On this night, I decided to get into the act—with my sister in the car. I don't even remember exactly what we did, but rest assured that it was really juvenile and stupid.

At some point, someone suggested that we should cover up my license plate in case our target tried to copy it down. Brilliant. It was trash day the next day, so everyone had their garbage cans out at the end of their driveway. We took part of a trash bag from someone's can and attached it to the license plates. There was no stopping us. We were criminal masterminds.

After the shenanigans, I dropped my sister off at home and went to my best friend's house to spend the night. At about 1:00 am, my friend's phone rang.

"Todd, the police are at your house," my friend said.

"Very funny," I replied.

"I'm serious, your mom just called."

I had known him since we were five years old. I usually had a pretty good idea when he was joking about something. I really wanted to believe he was joking about this—but he didn't seem to be joking.

I grabbed my stuff and drove home. He lived in the same neighborhood, so it only took about two minutes to drive home. It seemed like 20. As I pulled up to our house, sure enough, there was a police car parked on the street.

"Oh shit," I thought. Why couldn't my friend have been joking?

I walked in the front door. My stomach dropped, and I felt lightheaded. Standing there in a circle were two police officers, my mom, my dad, and my sister. My dad was in his underwear and a t-shirt (to this day I don't know why he didn't put pants on). His lips were clenched and his eyes were narrow. I knew this look. He was pissed. My sister had Clearasil dotting her distressed face. She looked as if her life was legitimately in danger. My mom had that look that moms have been perfecting since the beginning of time. Her mouth had a slight downturn, and her eyes were sad yet compassionate. It was a look that unmistakably and simultaneously let me know "I love you" and "I'm very disappointed in you." Also, "Your dad is pissed."

It was the two police officers whose faces were actually the most welcoming. They were almost smiling, like they wanted to pat me on the head out of sympathy. I think they knew that the fate that awaited me at home was far worse than anything they could dish out. The nice police officers explained that the man who lived at the house we'd visited had called and made a complaint that we were harassing him. Apparently, a piece of a garbage bag is not the license plate concealer that I thought it was. The cops handed me a ticket for disturbing the peace. And they left.

Our house was on a golf course. We didn't have a typical back yard with grass and a fence. Instead, it was a steep hill filled with trees, which led to the fairway of the fifth hole. It was basically a forest. We had a large deck that spanned the back of the house and looked out at the forest and fairway. This will become significant in a moment.

As soon as the door shut behind the police officers, my dad barked, "Give me your car keys."

Barely able to keep my hand steady, I reached into my pocket, pulled the keys out, and placed them in his hand. He told me to follow him. I had no idea where he was going, I just knew I needed to follow him. Still in his underwear, he marched across the family room, through the kitchen, and over to the door that opened to the deck. He threw the door open and, like an Olympian performing the javelin throw, reared back, took three or four shuffle steps, and heaved the keys off the deck into the night. I've never in my life—before or since then—seen him throw anything as far as he threw those keys that night. If the railing hadn't been there, he might have fallen off the deck.

"One month after you find those, come talk to me about driving again," he announced while pointing his finger at me. He marched past me back into his bedroom. I just stood there, dumbfounded, scared, and remorseful.

The first thing I did the next morning was look for those keys. I figured if I found them that day, I conceivably could be driving within a month. I did not find the keys. My dad told me years later that he thought he threw his arm out that night.

***

The disturbing-the-peace incident was not the only time my car got me in trouble. Actually, it was my car that was chiefly responsible for these messes, not me. One summer night when I was sixteen, I was with my friend Mike. (Are you sensing a pattern here with Mike?) In one of those classic teenage "what were you thinking?!" moments, we decided to take a stab at mailbox baseball. We drove to Mike's house, grabbed a bat, and went to work. Because we were teenagers and because teenagers do inherently stupid things, we decided to play said mailbox baseball *in my neighborhood*, mere blocks from where I actually lived and where neighbors knew me and my car. We decided it would be better for Mike to drive so I could be the designated hitter. We hit the first couple. I'm not sure that we did much damage. Honestly, I found it harder than I thought it would be to lean out the window, keep your balance, and lay a good swing on a mailbox. But I persisted.

We got to about our fourth or fifth target when, unbeknownst to us, there was a car sitting in a nearby driveway. The car was running with the driver inside, but its lights were off. After hearing the "whack!" of the wooden bat hitting the wooden mailbox, the guy sitting in the car decided to chase after us. My friend Mike, still driving, was more than willing to try to outrun this guy. Before I knew it, we were going 60 mph through my neighborhood streets. No neighborhood streets are designed for a 60-mph street race, but these streets were particularly winding and hilly. They weren't safe at 40 mph, let alone 60. It's a miracle we didn't get into an accident, or worse.

As a true testament to how utterly dumb the teenage brain can be, I remember thinking at the beginning of the chase, "Maybe it's a good thing Mike is driving, because there's no way I would have the balls to lead this guy on a chase through our neighborhood!" I would have pulled over right away and confessed the whole thing to the guy. "At least now we have a chance to get away with this!"

That didn't last long. Within a couple of seconds, I was paralyzed with fear.

"What the hell, Mike?! Slow down!!" I pleaded as I grabbed the door handle as hard as I could. My knuckles where white and my entire body was tense. You know what your body does on that amusement park ride that goes in circles until the bottom drops out and you're left sticking to the side because of the momentum of the ride? That's what my body looked like in the passenger seat.

"I got this," Mike replied, with the composure of a seasoned criminal who was also a NASCAR driver. His eyes calmly alternated between the rearview mirror and the road ahead, like we were on a Sunday drive. How many times had he done this before? Meanwhile, I was about to piss my pants like a little kid on a roller coaster.

After what seemed like 20 minutes, but was probably only a couple, we somehow lost the guy—or so we thought. Mike parked my car on the side of the street in our neighborhood (again, see the axiom that teenagers do stupid things). We stepped out of the car, not exactly sure of what to do next or where to go. The smell of burned rubber hit me right away. (To this day, whenever I smell that odor, I think of that night.) Our friend Brian lived about five minutes from where we'd parked. We decided to head there and took off at a jog. Fortunately, Brian was in the basement when we arrived, and we were able to sneak in rather than explain to his parents what we'd been doing out at 10:30 at night. Brian was confused when we showed up at the basement door out of breath.

"What are you guys doing?!"

"We need help," I said, breathing hard.

We explained the situation to him. He was amused and mystified at the mess we found ourselves in.

"What do you want me to do!?" he asked, perplexed.

We hadn't thought that far ahead. I had no idea what I wanted him to do. I think I wanted him to come up with something smart. He was one of the smartest kids at our school. I thought he would know what to do. Remarkably, he did not have a ready-made solution for us.

We left Brian's house, retreated to the nearby golf course, and hid. Mike eventually ran home. He didn't live in our neighborhood, but his house wasn't far from ours if you took back-road trails. I waited it out by myself on the golf course for a little while, then returned to my car and drove home. For a brief moment, it felt like we'd gotten away with it. I started to revel in the rush of the chase and getting away with something, although it was combined with the nagging pull of doing something destructive that I wasn't proud of.

The rush of the chase was short lived. Our pursuer had found my parked car. (Who knew it would be so easy to find, when we'd parked it in the same neighborhood as the chase?) He took down my license plate. (Should've used the trash bag again.) I'm not sure what exactly he did with the information, but whatever he did, something got back to my parents. While I managed to avoid a 1:00 am visit from the cops, I wasn't able to escape my parents' interrogation. Unable to summon Mike's lying super-power, I copped to the mailbox baseball immediately. There were no key heaves off the deck this time, but my dad was plenty pissed. I retreated to my room, where it felt like the walls were closing in on me. In that moment, to my teenage brain, it felt like I had just committed a first-degree felony and that my life would never be the same.

Suddenly, I remembered Mike's backpack. It had a two-liter bottle of Purple Passion in it. I didn't know if it was still in my car.

The ONE thing that was 100% guaranteed to get my car taken away for some time—between 20 years and forever—was to bring alcohol into it.

"Shit! I think it's still in the car! Did he take it with him?"

I didn't remember him carrying a backpack after we got out of my car.

"Why wouldn't he take it with him?!" On second thought, leaving it in my car was exactly what Mike would do, and something that would happen to me. Of course he'd left it in there!

I managed to sneak downstairs and outside to the driveway. I grabbed the Purple Passion from the backpack, walked around to the back of the house, and threw it into the trees behind our house. (It probably landed next to my car keys.)

My penance consisted of having to go to each house we'd vandalized, knock on the door, tell the owners what I'd done, then replace their mailbox or fix the damage. Before I did that, I had to go to the hardware store and buy new mailboxes, or supplies to fix the ones that didn't need replacing. I wondered whether the store employee we asked to help us knew why I was buying these mailboxes and supplies. I was ashamed and embarrassed. I felt two feet tall walking around that store.

I still remember stepping out of my mom's minivan and walking up the sidewalk to the front doors of those houses. I had a pit in my stomach so big it felt like I was going to throw up. The anxiety almost physically prevented me from ringing those doorbells.

When I mustered up the courage to actually speak to the home-owners, my voice was so unsteady I sounded like I was shivering. Most of the homeowners, bless their hearts, were incredibly warm and kind to me. My friend Mike offered to go with me and help me replace the mailboxes, but my mom and dad wouldn't let him do that unless he told his parents what we'd done—and there was a limit to Mike's desire to make amends.

My forays into stealing, disturbing the peace, and mailbox baseball taught me some valuable lessons and instilled in me that there were consequences to my actions. I had committed some fairly serious offenses. There should have been consequences. All that patting myself on the back for my quick thinking and lying to my mom about the tests, all that smugness and the adrenaline rush for thinking I'd gotten away with something—all that was wiped away, swiftly and permanently. That was good for me—I needed that. Would I have turned into a deadbeat or lifelong criminal if I hadn't been caught and learned those lessons? I doubt it, but it easily could have altered my path.

What I do know is that the rush of getting away with something is powerful stuff to a sixteen-year-old adolescent whose brain is not fully formed. Yes, I would have been wracked with guilt. But would that guilt, at some point, have been overridden by the rush of "getting away with it"? Maybe. Thankfully, it's a moot point, because instead of learning that I could get away with stuff like that, the ingrained, etched-in-my-mind-for-ever takeaway from those ordeals was that I had done something I knew was wrong. I'd gotten caught, I was embarrassed by it, and I suffered consequences. All this helped instill in me right versus wrong. My mom always would say, "Trust your gut," and these incidents helped drive that home. They also adjusted my compass to due north—something that (eventually) guided me when I started to confront my drinking issues.

The other thing it taught me was integrity. It taught me how important it was to do the right thing. Even when the right thing (turning your son in for stealing tests) is the hard thing. *Especially* when the right thing is the hard thing. As with most impactful lessons, I didn't appreciate all this in real time. As I got older and put more space between me and my lapses in judgment, and certainly since I've become a parent myself, that lesson has taken on new and greater significance. It also played a big part in my drinking journey.

CHAPTER FOUR

My Race to Nowhere

Some people remember their first drink of alcohol with the clarity and recall of a life-changing experience. I've heard people say they fell in love with alcohol at the first sip. It wasn't like that for me. I certainly remember the first time I got drunk (which was also the first time I drank), but it was not some "OMG, I have to have more of this" moment that sky-rocketed me into a life of overindulging. My path had a bit more arc to it.

I actually came to the drinking party pretty late in my adolescence. Most of my friends had been drinking for a couple of years by the time I finally indulged. In fact, I was one of those who would joke to my friends that alcohol wasn't necessary to have a good time. I wish I could say my stance at that time was based on principle and a desire simply to do the right thing and make the right decision, but it wasn't. My initial resistance to drinking came largely from my dad's drinking. Alcohol kind of scared me. People getting drunk made me feel unsettled and uneasy.

But by my junior year of high school the negative connotation I always had associated with drinking had been chipped away. I'd been around it enough, and nobody had died. Seeing my friends drunk did not leave me with the same unease as seeing my dad drunk did. Drinking seemed like so much more fun when they did it. It was much cooler. I looked on with a twinge of jealousy and envy as my friends laughed while they recounted stories of their drinking escapades. I wanted to be part of that. I wanted to tell my own stories. I wanted others to tell stories about me. Eventually, my unease and uncertainty gave way to curiosity to see what all the fuss was about, and to a desire to be part of it all. I was ready to give it a go.

The very first night I drank was at my best friend's house. His parents were gone for the night. They were smart enough to lock their liquor cabinet, but they weren't smart enough to put the key somewhere other than the cupboard directly next to the liquor cabinet. We drank some concoction of vodka, lemonade, and crushed ice that we made in a blender. All I remember is that the finished product tasted like a frozen lemonade drink. I didn't taste a bit of the vodka. I don't remember how many drinks I had. I'm sure one would have gotten me sufficiently drunk. I did get sufficiently drunk—and then some. At the time, I thought I liked the way it made me feel, but I think what I really liked was that people were talking about me. It made me feel like the center of attention—even if it was more along the lines of "OMG, look at Todd, he's drunk!" I didn't care, I just liked the attention. It also made me feel like I finally had joined the club. I was truly one of them now.

I never had felt unaccepted because I didn't drink, but I sure did feel more accepted once I did. It almost felt like a relief to shed the distinction of not drinking and whatever came along with that. It was like, "Okay, I gave the not-drinking thing a go, and it was fine. But now that I'm giving the drinking thing a go, it's better." I felt cooler, older, more mature (ha!), and more connected to my friends. At the end of the day, a lot of it was good old-fashioned peer pressure. And I don't mean direct pressure from my friends, because I don't remember it like that. I really don't remember people ostracizing me for not drinking. But subconsciously, the pressure was there. Maybe I put it all on myself. Maybe I invented some of it in my head. On some level, I felt the need to join my friends in this activity. It speaks to the overall subliminal messages we all receive about drinking even from a very young age. Because if I felt that pressure without being directly harassed by my friends, imagine how prevalent it is.

As an aside, remember when I told you I got caught for virtually everything I did wrong in high school? I'll let you guess whether my parents found out about the night at my best friend's house.

The rest of my high school drinking experiences were fairly typical. I like to think my friends and I were smart about drinking and didn't put ourselves in many situations where bad things could happen, and we were smart enough for that, for the most part. We mostly drank in small groups at someone's house. We generally took driving out of the equation. But we were still teenagers. We still did plenty of dumb things, and we're lucky that nothing terrible happened.

By the end of high school, I'd say I was a "normal" teenage drinker. I liked it. It still felt new and exciting. I thought about it a lot, but I just assumed that everyone else my age did too. In my mind, there was nothing to indicate at this point that my drinking was anything other than typical.

* * *

To the surprise of no one, after high school I attended the University of Iowa. It was the only college I applied to. I had wanted to go there ever since I started thinking about college. I had determined that it was the only place on earth I was going to attend college.

Before I go any further, let me explain a little bit about the role Iowa athletics plays in my life. I spend an inordinate amount of time, money, and energy on Iowa sports. I attended my first Iowa football game in 1981, when I was six years old. My dad took me. They were playing Nebraska. For some reason, it didn't hit me until the day of the game that I wasn't sure who to root for. I liked Iowa because my dad did. But I lived in Nebraska, so I sort of felt like I should root for them. (It's almost impossible to believe now that this was an actual dilemma!)

Nebraska was a powerhouse. Iowa hadn't had a winning season since 1961. 1961! My dad always said that when he went to school there, the loudest cheers came when Iowa got a first down. Hayden Fry had been hired as coach two years earlier and the program was showing signs of improvement. But still, Nebraska was ranked #6 in the country coming into the game and was a heavy favorite. Nobody expected Iowa to win the game. I don't remember this specifically, but knowing how kids are, I imagine that some of my hesitation about going all in on Iowa was that I assumed Nebraska was going to win. Kids like to back winners.

In a stunning upset, Iowa won the game, 10–7. The only thing I remember about the game is the crowd rushing the field after it was over. I had never seen that before. I had never seen that many people so happy. I'm not sure I had ever seen my dad that happy. Needless to say, I was hooked. I joke to my Nebraska friends that if Nebraska had just won that game, I probably would've grown up a Husker fan. But there was no going back for me. And so began what is now a 40-year journey that has brought me some of the greatest joy I've ever felt, the most agonizing heartbreak, the most intense frustration, and everything in between. There have been a few times I've cursed my Hawkeye fandom, but truth be told, I wouldn't change a thing. I cherish it.

My license plate reads HAWKS. I rarely leave the house without some sort of Iowa apparel on. I mark years by how Iowa did in football or basketball. Whenever someone brings up the year 1985, my first thought is always, "Iowa was ranked #1 for six weeks that year." When someone mentions 1987, I immediately think of the 1987–88 basketball team, one of Iowa's all-time best. They blew an eighteen-point halftime lead against UNLV with a trip to the Final Four on the line. It's the first time I remember crying over an Iowa game. I was devastated. I literally ran from the basement up to my bedroom, threw myself on my bed, and sobbed. I rewatch games and still get worked up over bad calls—even when I know Iowa ultimately won the game. I can remember the jersey numbers of players from 30 years ago. Same goes for scores of games decades ago. In comparison, I can't remember what I had for breakfast yesterday.

I played soccer from age five through high school. One of my earliest memories of playing isn't even a memory of a game itself. Instead, I remember coming off the field and checking with my dad about the score of the Iowa game. He was in the stands listening on his Walkman. I even remember who they played (Michigan) and what the final score was (a 9–7 win). I remember watching one of my first Iowa games on tv with my dad in 1985. When Chuck Long won the game on a last-second bootleg, Dad slapped me a high five so hard I thought my arm was going to come off. I thought he was acting kind of weird, he was so happy. And I remember how devastated I was when they lost to Ohio State later that year in the rain, which ruined their perfect season.

Todd Kinney

I was also a soccer referee growing up, which involved working on a lot of fall Saturdays. I would run over to my bag at halftime to put my Walkman on and find out what the score of the Iowa game was. About the only thing from third grade that I remember is writing a story about Rob Houghtlin's game-winning field goal that season to beat Michigan when Iowa was ranked #1 and Michigan was ranked #2. I've watched that highlight so many times over the years that I can recite the announcer's every word and describe the flight of the ball from the time it leaves Houghtlin's foot until it goes through the uprights.

While I was in high school, a popular Iowa basketball player named Chris Street was tragically killed in a car accident. I remember where I was when I found out, in the same way I remember where I was when the space shuttle exploded and when 9-11 happened. I cried when Hayden Fry retired in 1988. I cried when he passed away in December 2019. I will cry when Kirk Ferentz retires.

While at Iowa, I wore the same sweatshirt to every football game. That sweatshirt is now autographed by Hayden Fry and hangs behind a glass case in our basement. My junior year of college, I took the LSAT on a fall Saturday. Iowa had a home football game, and the LSAT did not get over until after the game started. I can't tell you anything about the LSAT that day, but I remember running across campus to get to Kinnick Stadium for the second half (and stopping at a convenience store to pick up the biggest bottle of beer I could buy), I remember who we played (Michigan State), and I remember the outcome of the game (Iowa stormed back from a thirteen-point halftime deficit). Needless to say, I ended up with a very average LSAT score.

I hesitate even to admit this, but part of how I remember that 2002 is the year I got married is because that was Iowa's Orange Bowl season, in which they finished 8–0 in the conference. I know when my father-in-law turned 60 because his party was during the Iowa–Northwestern game in 2009, when Iowa was ranked #4 in the country but lost for the first time that season. I know when my wife turned 30 because it was the day before Iowa's most dramatic bowl win ever, when they won on the last play of the game with a 56-yard touchdown pass. I can recite the radio announcer's call of that play in my sleep.

In 2015, I attended the Iowa–Minnesota game. Iowa won to move to 10–0 for the first time in school history. After the game, I sat at a table in my favorite dive bar and cried. To clarify, I wasn't sobbing or making a scene. That would be embarrassing! But as I sat in my favorite bar—one that's been around for so long that my dad went there when he was a student at Iowa—and thought about how Iowa had just done something it never had done before, I cried a few tears of happiness.

Later that year, Iowa was 12–0 and played in the Big Ten championship in Indianapolis. The atmosphere around Indy the day leading up to that game was unlike any I've ever seen before. Iowa fans were everywhere. A win would have put Iowa into the college football playoffs. They lost in heartbreaking fashion, after Michigan State scored in the final two minutes after a nine-plus-minute march down the field. I physically hurt after that game. (I know, it sounds ridiculous—it is a little ridiculous—but it's true. What can I say?) I once sat in the dark in our family room for about 45 minutes just staring into space after Iowa lost a Big Ten tournament game to Michigan State that cost them an NCAA tourney bid. Now that I think about it, Michigan State is responsible for some dark days in my life.

After Iowa started the 2020 season (the COVID year) 0–2, I switched up my gameday shirt and sweatshirt. They went 6–0 after that, and I sincerely believe my change of wardrobe played a role in the turnaround.

I estimate that I've been to approximately 120 home football games. I've been to countless road games and eleven bowl games. I've been to home and away basketball games and traveled to follow Iowa in the NCAA tournament. I've been fortunate enough to attend all four Rose Bowls that Iowa has played in during my lifetime (and zero wins!). In 2015, I was able to take three of my kids to the Rose Bowl. My dad went too. Iowa got absolutely mauled by Stanford, but it was one of the best trips of my life. To be able to go to the Rose Bowl with three of my kids and my dad? Now that was special!

As my friends will tell you—while rolling their eyes—I can take just about any story about any topic and turn it back to something Iowa-related. If I knew half as much about the law as I do Iowa sports, I would be a Supreme Court justice. Yes, I take Iowa sports too seriously. Yes, it affects my mood more than it should. And no, I wouldn't change a thing. I will love the Hawks until the day I die.

Todd Kinney

As you might have guessed, I never really had a decision to make when it came to college. I remember my sister Kristin going through a much more difficult and tortured process of picking a college a year later—mostly because she was a great soccer player and accomplished student. She had several attractive options, so it was a difficult decision for her. It was so foreign to me that someone would have to spend so much time and energy deciding where to go to college.

* * *

The summer before I left for college, my future roommate and I went to Iowa City for orientation, which involved an overnight stay in the dorms. A couple of guys down the hall invited us to their room to hang out. They had a case of beer, which they shared with us. I don't remember how many I had or how many my friend had, but I bet I had twice as many beers as he did and got twice as drunk. Most people in a situation like that—when you're meeting people for the first time, when you're in a new setting, when you want to make a good impression—would be extra cautious about their drinking. They'd be aware of all those things and would monitor their drinking accordingly. Not me. It was almost the opposite for me. I felt like I had to get to that place, that buzz, before I felt truly comfortable—or thought I felt comfortable.

What I remember about that night—and this is something that came to define my drinking from that point forward—was the urgency I felt to get drunk. It was as if that case of beer represented the last drops of alcohol on the planet. I absolutely could not let this opportunity go to waste. I was in a hurry, singularly focused on getting a buzz, on getting to an altered state. Everything else was secondary. The people I was with, the scenery, the conversations—it all took a back seat. It was like a race for me. A race where I didn't have time to look up and figure out how drunk I was getting. I had this nagging feeling that I had to hurry up and get somewhere. It was a Race to Nowhere.

Once I got to that point, any ability I had to moderate my drinking (which was minimal to begin with) was reduced even further. My inhibitions dropped. My willpower faded. The determination with which I started the day was chipped away by each sip. As the night wore on, I

26

became less and less concerned about keeping it in check. Keeping it in check is so much damn work! Who wants to work that hard when you're trying to have fun? And so went the Race.

This sequence played out in my head almost every time I drank. It went something like this:

> Don't drink too much today. You know how that can ruin things and how shitty you feel afterward.
>
> I won't. I want this to be a good day. I am NOT going to let things get out of control.
>
> [Orders first drink; starts thinking about the second.]
>
> Oh man, that beer tastes good. I'm ready for another.
>
> Watch yourself.
>
> I don't need to watch myself yet. It's only #2.
>
> [Orders next drink; starts to feel buzzed.]
>
> Okay, I should probably think about slowing down.
>
> Oh, someone is going to the bar for another round? Okay, I'll take another. (I mean, if I don't, then I might have to wait another 20 minutes for the next drink. And that just can't happen).
>
> Okay, after this one, time to get serious about slowing down.

The idea of just drinking a little or (gasp!) not drinking at all did not even enter my thought process. That was like asking me, "Did you give any thought to amputating your arm that night?" Why would anyone give any thought to something like that?

I was obsessed with when and where my next drink was coming from. If I went longer than three minutes in between finishing one drink and starting another, something bad was going to happen. I wasn't entirely sure what, I just knew it would be bad, or that it felt like it would be bad. It was like cutting off my oxygen. The mere idea of it was anxiety-inducing. The relief of securing that next drink was palpable. That's why, when my drink was about halfway done, I started planning for the next one. I'd look around to check where everyone else was at. If I saw someone whose drink was almost empty, that was an in for me. "Oh, look, they're almost done. Good! They'll need to order another drink, and I might as well get a refill while the server is here." My Race to Nowhere usually had only one participant and no winners.

I always could find a justification for cutting loose. All it took was one person. I could be in a room full of 25 people who were all drinking normally, and if I saw one person who looked like he was hitting it hard, then boom! There's my excuse. Oh, look at John, he's getting after it tonight. Well then, so can I! I'm not the only one! John and I are in this together! (Never mind that John probably wasn't even getting after it like I thought he was).

A night out felt like a failure, a waste, if I didn't get sufficiently drunk. On nights where I drank a "normal" amount of alcohol, yes, part of me would be proud of myself for keeping it in check. But somewhere inside me there would be this nagging annoyance that I hadn't drunk more. Almost like it wasn't a "real" experience. Drinking in moderation was something that some people did (apparently some even did it on a regular basis) that I was just "trying on" for a night. But looking back, those nights felt weird. Of course, I liked feeling as if I'd accomplished something, and I loved the fact that I didn't feel regret or shame over my drinking. But if I'm being completely honest, it didn't feel like me. I felt kind of like a fraud doing that. It's like when you eat someone else's terrible cooking and you put a smile on your face and tell them it tastes good. Only, I was merely trying to convince myself that I liked this type of drinking. Actually I did like it; I just wasn't sure that it was worth the work. More often than not, I used the nights I kept it under control as an excuse to cut loose the next night.

My "baseline" became most people's "drunk." When I drank, I didn't really "start" until I had a buzz going. So if the usual idea is to have a drink or two while watching a game at home, my idea was to have enough drinks to get that buzz, then take it from there. Once that buzz hit, it was almost impossible for me to stop. Why would you stop then? It would be like starting to have sex and then deciding to stop before you have an orgasm.

I got so used to being in that buzzed state yet acting like I wasn't that it became second nature. I become quite good at it—probably not as good as I thought I was, but after doing it so many times, I forgot that it's not really normal. It became *my* normal. But not everyone else's. So that's what I identified with drinking: drinking = buzzed. That's part of the reason why drinking one beer was hardly ever enough for me. Drinking one beer didn't get me buzzed, so why on earth would anyone ever drink just one?

That night at orientation was so cool. Here I was at age eighteen, on my own for the night in a dorm, meeting interesting people from different states. And doing it over beers! It felt so grown up, so adult. I felt like I had crossed some imaginary threshold into a new, sophisticated, worldly existence. I found the whole thing intoxicating, for lack of a better word. It left me invigorated. I was *so* ready for college.

***

My very first night as full-fledged college student, I threw up in my bed. At around 10 pm. I don't even remember where we got the alcohol or what we did. I just remember I was the only one in our group who got really drunk. My usual sense of urgency kicked in, and I ran my Race to Nowhere. I ended up also puking on my roommate's shoes. Luckily, I knew him from high school. While he wasn't thrilled with how our college experience started off, he didn't disown me either. So my first night at college was spent in the laundry room, drunk, washing my sheets. I was off to an awesome start.

Not surprisingly, I became that guy at college who always got really drunk. One of the big traditions at Iowa (and it's hardly unique to that university) was to go out early on Friday afternoons. When I was there, you could get into a bar at age nineteen, but you couldn't drink (yeah, right). So the bars were popular hangouts on Friday afternoons. Most people would go to the bars in the afternoon, then go home and get ready to go out for the night. But more often than not, I wouldn't make it out at night because I drank so much in the afternoon.

During my junior year of college, I studied abroad in Edinburgh, Scotland, for a semester. One of the first weekends we were there, we spent with a host family. Mine was in northern England. The family I stayed with had five kids, one of whom was a sixteen-year-old boy. He and two of his friends took me to a club one night. The evening itself was uneventful. We all drank, but I didn't drink an absurd amount. Still, I remember falling asleep on the ride home, when nobody else did. I woke up when we stopped at a gas station, fell asleep again, then woke up again when we dropped the friends off. Here I was at 20 years old, out with three sixteen-year-olds—who all handled their alcohol better than I did.

I remember the first time I was confronted with the fact that the way I thought about alcohol might not be normal. I had gotten into the habit of having a beer when I got done studying for the night. Sometimes this was at 8:00 pm, sometimes it was at 11:00 pm. But whenever it was, I always wanted a drink before I turned in for the night. I looked forward to it. It felt like a reward after a long night of studying (even if it wasn't necessarily a long night of studying). It helped me unwind, I told myself. I'll sleep better with that beer. Isn't sleep important?! So I'd better have that beer.

One night, I went back to my girlfriend's place when we were done studying. The boyfriend of one of her roommates was at the house when we got there. Everyone was getting ready to go to bed for the night when I walked out of the kitchen opening a bottle of beer. The boyfriend looked at me like I had three heads. "Man, it's 11:30, what are you doing opening a beer?!" I wasn't fully prepared for the inquisition, so I didn't have a sensible response ready (is there a sensible response?) I mumbled something about just winding down after a long day, but what I really wanted was to get the spotlight off me as quickly as possible. I felt like everyone in the room was staring at me, thinking, "Yeah, Todd, why ARE you having a beer at 11:30 at night?" They were just looking at me, waiting for me to respond. Everything else was quiet. I could feel each set of eyes on me, evaluating and judging my decision to have a beer and, even worse, judging me as a person who would do such a thing.

"It's just ONE beer! Relax! It doesn't mean I have a problem!" I felt like screaming, just to get these people off my back. Luckily for me, the boyfriend did not stay at the house very often.

One of my most vivid memories from college is watching someone on our floor freshman year get wheeled out on a stretcher because of alcohol poisoning. His dorm room was a couple doors down from ours. As you might imagine, the incident created quite a scene on our floor. We had a resident assistant, but other than him, there was nobody to keep the crowd away. The doorway was narrow, but that didn't stop the crowd from trying to peer inside. I stood on my tiptoes and stretched my neck, trying to see what was going on inside, even though I wasn't totally sure I wanted to. Slowly the stretcher was wheeled out of the room. It passed right in front of me as I backed up against the cold, concrete wall to make room for the EMTs to pass by. I could have reached out and touched him. He was on oxygen. He didn't look awake; his eyes were open, but they looked blank. I had a knot in my stomach. It seemed like the EMTs should be rushing more. I took an odd sense of comfort in the fact that they weren't. Still, I felt unnerved and scared.

Whenever something like that happens—a medical emergency, a fight, a car accident—a distinct feeling comes over me. It's a mix of adrenaline and fear—fight or flight. But there's also a lingering malaise that hangs over me after the initial rush of fear and adrenaline, something that sticks with me like a cloud over my head. It's hard to shake. It's an uneasy feeling that prevents me from feeling "normal" for a while. It's like my mind is not letting me move on until I have sufficiently processed what I've just seen, or tried to. I had that feeling with this incident.

But that entire scene, and the nagging unease that stuck around, had zero effect on my drinking. It should have jolted me into evaluating something about the way I drank, so it wouldn't be me the next time that stretcher got wheeled out of our dorm. But the experience didn't have that effect, not even for a second. Instead, my takeaway was, "I might get too drunk sometimes, but at least I've never gotten alcohol poisoning. My drinking isn't *that* bad." The extent of my awareness at the time was along the lines of, "Yeah, sometimes I drink too much. I should do something about that." I did want to do something about it, but this wasn't much different from saying "I should work out more" or "I should save more money."

There were a few occasions when I easily could have been that guy on the stretcher. One night at a fraternity party, I spent part of the night sitting by a fireplace puking on myself. A band was playing. People were dancing, talking, and drinking all around me. Eventually I made it back to my dorm room across the street, with help from a couple of friends. I could have been the guy on a stretcher that night. There were other nights when we started drinking early on Friday afternoon, and I would be passed out by 5:00 pm. The morning after one of those nights, a friend told me he and others had been worried about me because of how drunk I was, and that I didn't seem to be very responsive before passing out the night before. I could have been the guy on the stretcher that night. The only difference between the guy on the stretcher and me was that someone chose to call 911 for the guy on the stretcher. I wish those nights had been few and far between, but they weren't.

The issues that plagued my whole drinking career were all there in college. All too often, I was the drunkest one in the room. I didn't have the "off" switch that most people have. I drank fast. I spent an inordinate amount of time thinking about drinking. And the morning after I would experience shame, embarrassment, and regret. College was the starting line for my Race to Nowhere.

The fun lasted for four years. By the time I graduated from college, I knew I would be going to law school, I just didn't know where. I thought, law school will be a less-fun, more-serious version of college. Surely I'll have to grow up and start drinking less like a college student and more like a responsible adult.

CHAPTER FIVE

The Party Continues

I had wanted to go to law school ever since I started thinking about what to be when I grew up. In third grade, I took a summer school class on the legal system. It culminated with us putting on a mock trial in a real courtroom. I loved everything about that class. I especially loved being in the courtroom and arguing "my" case. I thought it was so cool to be doing that in a real courtroom in front of a real judge (actual judges volunteered to hear the cases). It may as well have been a U.S. Supreme Court argument, as far as I was concerned. I was hooked. Other than a brief spell when I studied abroad, when I thought about being a sports agent, I never really deviated from that path.

This time my school choice was not based on a fanatical devotion to any sports team. Quite the opposite, actually—I ended up going to the University of Nebraska for law school. I assumed that law school would involve less drinking than college had. I thought, "It's graduate school. It's more serious than college." Time to buckle down and take it even more seriously than I had taken college. I remember wondering whether people dressed nicer for class in law school; I figured they did. The idea of a law school professor seemed more "serious" than just a "regular" college professor. Plus, I was past the college phase. That was in the rear-view mirror. Law school was a serious step toward a real, professional life. Wasn't it time to start behaving a little differently?

The short answer is no. One of my first realizations about law school was that drinking was pretty much a "sanctioned" activity. In college, even though drinking was everywhere, there always had been the notion that the university was looking over your shoulder. The school's official stance (even though it made little difference) was that "drinking is bad." In law school, it seemed to be, "Welcome to law school, where people drink a lot, and that's just the way it is." Right before classes started, the student bar association hosted a party with an open bar. Everyone got hammered. It was no different than a college party. There was even a professor there, who seemed to drink as much as the students. "Holy shit," I thought. "This is my kind of place!"

Law school can drive many to drink, but it can be particularly fraught with landmines for someone who already has drinking issues. It's the perfect storm of factors that can exacerbate drinking. First, if you could overdose on imposture syndrome, I probably would have done so in law school. I was surrounded by high achievers, people who had done very well in college and life in general. I think it's natural for everyone to look around and think, "Do I really belong here?" My college GPA and my LSAT score were dead average compared with those of my classmates, so I certainly couldn't draw much inspiration there. I always thought that I would perform well in law school because it was something I was passionate about, but that only took me so far when everywhere I looked I saw someone with an impressive resumé whom I was convinced was smarter than me. On my best day, I thought, "Okay, maybe I can hold my own here." On my worst day, I thought I 'd been granted admission because of some administrative mistake that eventually would be discovered, and I would be ushered out the door by the dean while the entire class watched and laughed. Most days in between, I would go back and forth, trying to convince myself that I did, indeed, belong there.

That internal battle got old. Sometimes I didn't even realize that it was raging inside me. It also made me want to drink. When I was getting drunk with my classmates, I felt like I *did* belong, and that felt good. It paused the internal back and forth of trying to convince myself that I was good enough for law school. That also felt good.

Law school is also stressful in itself. That's not a news flash. But I had no awareness at the time of the effects that stress would have on my drinking. In law school, there are no grades throughout the semester. You simply go to class, do a shitload of reading, pray that you don't get called on in class and cross-examined by the professor, then pray that you don't shit your pants when you do get called on in class, and wonder if you're learning what you're supposed to be learning along the way. There's no feedback. There are no tests or quizzes along the way to reinforce the way you're studying or let you know that you need to start doing something different. You're flying blind. On top of all that, you're learning in a way (the Socratic method) that's completely different from anything you've ever experienced before. You never know whether you're doing things right until you take a single exam at the end of the semester. Often, that one exam determines your entire grade for the class. That makes finals slightly stressful.

Stress, of course, results in drinking. Or at least it did for me at that point (and for a long time afterward). I had no other way of releasing the stress or dealing with it. I had worked out in college, but on and off, not all that seriously. In law school, I didn't do much other than play pickup basketball or intramural flag football. And I didn't use those activities as a stress-management tool. So my list of stress-relieving activities was a short one. It looked like this:

1) drinking.

Combined with the fact that this was true for most of my classmates (or at least the ones I hung out with), I never really gave it a second thought.

I didn't experience any spectacular embarrassments with my drinking in law school. That's not to say I didn't have cringe-worthy moments, because I did.

One night during my first year, I went back to the apartment of the girl I was dating at the time. I had been out at the bars and was about "average" drunk for me, which is to say I was "above average" drunk for the normal person. The woman I was dating at the time was a great person. We had an on-again/off-again relationship—mostly because I didn't have my shit together in my personal life. She deserved better than what I was giving her at the time. Anyway, I walked in the door, took my shoes off—

and we promptly got into an argument. I have no idea what it was about, but most likely something stupid. I have little doubt that my intoxication made the argument worse.

And I have no doubt that the next thing I said made things even worse: "Come on, Lisa," I said, pleading with her to stop being mad about whatever it was.

The problem was, her name wasn't Lisa. My ex-girlfriend's name was Lisa, though. The current girlfriend promptly picked up my shoes, walked out to her apartment's balcony, and threw them from the third floor down onto the parking lot. Apparently, she wanted me to leave. So I sat on the curb in the parking lot, called a friend to come pick me up, and went home with my tail between my legs. I'm happy to report that this girlfriend wised up, moved on from me, and has been married to a great guy (a friend of mine) for about 20 years. I hope he never calls her Lisa.

***

In law school, we had our own version of "senior superlatives." Some were the traditional, normal type: "Most likely to serve on the Supreme Court." "Smartest." "Best in a courtroom." "Most likely to be a law school professor." Others were more light-hearted and designed to be funny. "Most likely to need a criminal lawyer." "Most likely to sleep with a client."

The person in charge of the senior superlatives gave me a heads up that I was on track to "win" the "most likely to sleep with a client" title. I wasn't sure how I felt about that. Part of me felt like these things were just for fun, nobody took them that seriously, and they didn't really mean anything. Ha ha, it's just something we do at the end of a grueling three years to have some fun, something to laugh about. Nobody remembers these things anyway. That's what I told myself over and over.

The other part of me—the one that nagged away in the back of my mind, and the part that I tried to quiet down—didn't like "winning" this title. What does that say about what my classmates think of my morals and ethics? Sleeping with a client is a disbarrable offense! Do they really think I would do something like that? I'm not sure I like that that they think of me that way. However, at the time I never went too deep with these feelings—I didn't want to.

There was also the matter of my then-girlfriend, who is now my wife. What would she think? At the time, I honestly didn't think she would consider it a big deal. Now, that sounds naïve and stupid. But remember, at the time I was working hard to convince myself that this was all in good fun and nobody took it seriously, instead of examining what it really might mean. So, one day, as casually as I could, I brought it up.

"You know those stupid senior superlative things? Someone told me I might win the 'most likely to sleep with a client' award." I said, waiting for her to casually laugh it off and let me off the hook.

"Are you fucking kidding me?" she scoffed. She shook her head in disgust and started to walk away. It looked like she was on the verge of crying.

Uh oh. So much for her thinking this wasn't a big deal. I felt like shit—both for "winning" the award and for thinking that it wouldn't be a big deal to her. I knew I had to do something.

I tracked down the guy in charge of the superlatives, Tom. Tom was a studious, straitlaced guy who didn't exactly set out to break rules. Still, I figured that if I laid it all on the line for him he would understand my predicament and help me out.

"Listen, I have a problem. Beth got very upset when I told her I might win this award. She was about to start crying. This is going to cause a lot of problems for me if I win. Can't you just give it to Matt?"

Matt was in second place, or so I heard. He seemed like the kind of guy who actually might *like* to win the award.

Tom's face remained motionless while I was pleading my case. No nodding, no smiling. I was desperately searching for something to indicate that he was somewhat sympathetic to my dilemma, but I was getting nothing, and it was making me anxious.

"Nobody will know! It's a victimless crime." I was close to pleading by now.

"I don't know," was all he said, with the same expressionless face.

"Dude, it's not a big deal! Nobody is ever going to know," I said. I was full-on pleading now.

"I don't know," he repeated.

Well, great. I didn't like my chances that Tom would bail me out. So I decided to take matters into my own hands.

Todd Kinney

The way we voted on the superlatives was that everyone received a "ballot" in their law school mailbox. The ballot was a piece of paper with the superlatives hand-written on it, with a blank for you to fill in your vote. After you filled yours out, you dropped it in Tom's mailbox. The ballots were anonymous. I took a blank ballot, made several photocopies, and then filled in the "most likely to sleep with a client" blank with names other than my own—including several with Matt's name. I didn't put his name on all of them because, well, I thought that would look too suspicious. I then dropped the additional ballots in Tom's mailbox.

For the record, the thought did cross my mind to fill in my name for some of the more-prestigious awards on these fake ballots. I thankfully had the good sense to refrain. For one, people definitely would have believed that something was up with the integrity of the process if I had won "most likely to be a Supreme Court justice." Two, karma would've gotten me somehow—I'm convinced of that. What I was doing to save my own ass was bad enough, but to do that AND cheat to win one of the awards that people actually wanted to win? That was low.

I ended up not "winning" the title. I don't know for sure whether my ballot-stuffing was the reason, but I suspect it was. Interestingly, I saw Matt at a law school alumni function several years later. I don't remember the details of the conversation—partly because I was drinking and partly because I tried to rush past it as fast as possible—but he made an offhand remark that let me know he had a pretty good idea of what I'd done. It was one of those comments where he was *mostly* joking and laughing about it, but it also was tinged with just enough sharpness for him to let me know that he wasn't completely cool with it. I never told Beth what I did.

I'm still not comfortable with what that award said about how my classmates viewed me. I don't like thinking about it, but I've examined it more. For a long, long time, my first reaction was always to be defensive about it. "Why did they think that? There's no reason for them to think that." My first year of law school, the only girl I dated was the one who threw my shoes off the balcony. We were on and off a lot, which certainly didn't help me win over her friends. But I never cheated on her. For some reason, I connected cheating on a girlfriend or partner with behavior that would lead someone to vote me most likely to sleep with a client.

My second year was when I met Beth. She was a year behind me. We certainly had a rocky start, with a few starts and stops (not all my fault this time!). But again, there was no cheating. So what the hell? Why would my classmates think I deserved to win that award? In a sense, it bothers me more today than it did at the time. At age 25, with very little experience in the "real world" of law, the idea of sleeping with a client was more of an abstract thing. Yes, of course, I knew that it's something you should not do. But it was kind of like, "Of course it's wrong, but what if…?" It was negotiable under certain circumstances—or it seemed like it *might* be. It was something you could maybe, possibly, kind of talk yourself into. As with most things in life, I didn't have the appreciation or the perspective to understand what a serious offense it was. As I got older, it became "there are no what-ifs" on this one. There just aren't. So, in that sense, it bothers me more today.

But I also still harken back to where we were at the time. I wasn't receiving this award as someone who had been practicing law for 20 years. I was receiving at is a 25-year-old getting ready to graduate from law school. And I was being awarded it by other kids getting ready to graduate. I'd like to think that nobody would vote for me today. But I still don't like that I was the person most people wanted to write in on that line at the time. It still makes me cringe. My reflex is still to make the thought go away whenever it pops into my head. I wish I hadn't done what I did with the ballots. I wish the whole thing never happened.

I can't help but think that I never would have been in the running for that award if I didn't drink in law school. My drinking hadn't changed much from college to law school. This "award" boils down to integrity—or a lack of it. Nothing quite chips away at integrity, both internally and in others' perceptions, like drinking too much. It doesn't matter that you strive to live a life of integrity otherwise. Drinking always provides an asterisk.

***

There's something uniquely torturous about the legal field in that, even after suffering through three years of grueling schooling, feeling like you don't know anything, and questioning every bit of your intellectual capability, but earning that diploma, you're *still* not certified to practice law yet. That, of course, requires one last test that you spend half the summer preparing for. A summer that, if you're like me, is driven as much by fear of failure as anything else.

Every lawyer has a story about where they were when they found out they'd passed the bar exam. Back in 2000, we still got our results via regular old snail mail. We got our results on a Friday. A friend called me one morning to say that the results would come out that day. From that moment on, my stomach was in knots. I couldn't think about anything else. I couldn't eat or concentrate. At the time, I was clerking at the law firm where I now work. I did my best to have normal conversations with people that morning, I could see their mouths moving and hear sounds coming out, and I was nodding along, but their words were not registering with me.

At the time, I lived in an apartment about a half mile from the office. All the building's mailboxes were on the first floor. I walked by them every time I entered the building. I had a vague idea of when the mail came every day. About an hour before that, I left work and went home. For some reason, I thought the suspense of it all would be easier to handle from home. I was wrong.

About 30 minutes before the earliest possible time the mail would have arrived, I began checking the mailboxes every five minutes or so. Finally, on what must have been my fifth trip, I saw the mailman walking out of the building. It was time. I already had my mailbox key separated from the other keys on my key ring. It didn't take me long to find the envelope with the "Supreme Court of the State of Nebraska" on it. I didn't open it there. I took the stairs two at a time back up to my apartment, where I could open it in privacy—just in case.

The knots in my stomach intensified. I felt like the slightest of odd smells or tastes would make me throw up. My hands were not steady. My brain was going a million miles an hour. What if I'd failed? What would I tell people? How would I tell them? What would my excuse be? What about my job? When was the soonest I could take the test again? I momentarily convinced myself that every minute of studying I'd endured had been unproductive and a waste of time. Surely all that studying hadn't been a waste, though, right? Right?! But I'd never been a great standardized test taker. I suddenly was engulfed in a wave of self-doubt, self-sabotage, and despair.

I tried to open the envelope but couldn't slide my finger across the top horizontally, my normal way of opening letters. After fumbling for a second, I tore the entire end of the envelope open. I could see that inside was a notecard that didn't take up the width of the entire envelope, so I didn't have to worry about tearing any of the contents. The bar exam is divided into two parts, multiple choice and essay, and each one is scored separately. You have to score a certain level on each part to pass. The threshold changes each year depending on how everyone who takes the test does. The notecard listed the threshold score on top and my score right below (multiple choice on the left side of the card, essay on the right side). The plainness of the notecard betrayed the magnitude of the information contained on it.

I have no idea what my score on either section was. All I know is that each number on the bottom was higher than the threshold score on the top. I rechecked a couple of times to make sure, like I had just won the lottery and was making sure the numbers actually matched. My mind was racing, and I wanted to be sure I wasn't making a mistake. Once I confirmed that I wasn't, I pumped my fists and let out a scream that was equal parts pure, unfiltered joy and utter relief. I danced around my apartment by myself. I celebrated as if Iowa had just won a national title. I felt so much lighter. The stress and self-doubt of the prior three years felt like they melted away all at once. I was proud of myself. The first call I made was to my dad.

It was just a given that I would get shitfaced on this day (whether I passed or not!). It was preordained. It was also a given that I would remember little from it. Never in a million years did it occur to me to do anything different. Usually, prior to a night of drinking, I would give some amount of thought and effort to keeping it under control. I would give myself the familiar pep talk:

"Now, don't ruin tonight by getting too drunk. You know what can happen, and you know you'll regret it in the morning. Let's keep it under control."

On this day, giving that talk to myself was like putting a bowl full of candy in front of a child and telling him not to eat too much. Keep it under control? I just passed the bar! So did a bunch of my friends! Fuck that! We're partying tonight!

I'd known for months how that night would turn out. I probably remember less than half the night. I got so drunk I couldn't enter the code to get into my apartment building when I came home.

It seems so foolish when I think about it now. Why would I deliberately go out and do something that (1) would inevitably make it more likely that I wouldn't remember the day and (2) would almost guarantee that I would attach some shame and regret to it all? I mean, I get it. I know exactly what I was thinking and feeling at the time. I had a great excuse to go out and drink a lot. To drink like I wanted to. Those occasions were like Christmas for me. It's acceptable to do that after you pass the bar, right? At least it's less unacceptable. It's kind of, sort of, a free pass to get as shitfaced as you want. Or in my case, to just drink without worrying about the guardrails. That's an opportunity that you have to run with. It's also a sure-fire way to turn what should be a celebratory milestone in your life into something that's tainted forever. Now that I think about it, that pretty well sums up alcohol's role in my life for many years.

CHAPTER SIX

Seeds of Change

My dad quit drinking in 2001. Not because he thought he had a problem, but because my mom thought he did. There were only two times when my dad wondered to himself whether he had an issue with drinking. One was when he and some of his siblings traveled to see his brother in a rehab facility out of town. One of the employees there told my dad and his siblings that they were not allowed to drink the entire weekend, including when they were away from the facility itself. My dad thought that was bullshit. "This guy can't tell me what I can do on my own," he thought. And to prove it, he and his sister drank while they were not at the facility. Still, he was bothered by how much the drinking prohibition bothered him. It struck him that that might mean something.

The other time his drinking gave him some pause was when his beloved great aunt was dying. He was very close to her. One night, he and his parents gathered at her bedside. She was passing away but, as those things often go, nobody knew whether it was going to happen in a couple hours or a couple days. It was getting late, they had been there a while, and my dad wanted a drink. He suggested to his parents that they go get one and then call it a night. So they did. His great aunt passed away a few hours later. It still nags at him today that he wasn't by her side because he wanted to go home and have a drink.

At one point, in an effort to prove to my mom that he didn't have a problem, he underwent an evaluation by a trained drug-and-alcohol counselor. She interviewed him and he answered the questions as honestly as any of us do. Which is to say, mostly true but probably not the entire story. The counselor gave him a clean bill of health. He had a lot going on between his demanding job and helping to raise four kids. All that, according to the counselor, was enough of a guardrail on his drinking that it wasn't deemed problematic. He had his shit together, so drinking wasn't a problem. She did tell him to keep an eye on things once retirement rolled around. That minor concern aside, he walked out of that evaluation with his arms raised in the air like Rocky walking down the steps of the Philadelphia Museum of Art. "See! I told you! I'm fine," he could tell my mom.

My mom wasn't convinced. I never saw her nag my dad about his drinking. She never said a word to us kids about it when we were growing up. She never gave him an ultimatum. A big part of her dealing with my dad's drinking was shielding us kids from it. Planning around it. How would the babysitter get home? Were we going to be up when they got home? Could she get my dad to the bedroom without seeing any of us? How would she explain his behavior if we saw him?

By 2001, my dad still didn't think he had a problem. But the fact that my mom did was weighing on him. It was weighing on *them*. He felt like she was losing patience. What better way to prove to her that he didn't have a drinking problem than to give it up for Lent? Can anyone with a drinking problem give up alcohol for 40 nights? No way. So my dad gave it up for Lent that year, setting out to prove to my mom, once and for all, that he didn't have a drinking problem. It was hard, but he was extremely determined. He knew he couldn't slip up, or he'd be wrong and my mom would be right. He was desperate to prove that he was right.

But along the way, he started noticing that he was waking up without any anxiety. The pressures of work—which were relentless and heavy— eased. The headaches were gone. The hangovers that had intruded far into the day after disappeared. He was sleeping better. He had more energy. There was so much good that came with not drinking.

For my dad, the best part of not drinking was how proud my mom was of him—he loved it. He had so much support from my mom. She bought him flowers almost weekly to celebrate the latest milestone. He didn't want to throw that away. And he loved how proud of himself he was too.

He woke up on Easter morning in 2001 and thought, "Why would I give up all this good stuff?" He hasn't had a drink since.

I was 26 when my dad quit. On the one hand, I was surprised, because *nobody* liked drinking as much as my dad did. I was not privy to any internal battle he had going on or how much it was weighing on him that my mom thought he had a problem. In that sense, the change came out of the blue. But part of me wasn't surprised, because when my dad puts his mind to something he usually ends up doing it.

I'm certain that his quitting had a lot to do with me ultimately deciding to give it up too. The further I get from my drinking days, the clearer that becomes. I'm a lot like my dad in many ways, including in my drinking. Even though I was not a nightly drinker by the time I gave it up for good, we drank similarly. The very first thing I thought after finding out that he was giving it up for good was, "Oh shit, I'm going to have to do this too someday, aren't I?" I chased that thought away as fast as it came in, so it wouldn't linger and prompt any serious self-evaluation. That thought showing up, even though I didn't do anything about it for a long time, started the process that eventually led me to where I am today. A seed had been planted, even if I didn't know it at the time.

The other thing about my dad quitting that was so meaningful for me was that by the time I started contemplating giving it up for good, I knew that if my dad had done it and lived to tell about it, I could too. At the time, I hardly knew anyone personally who had given up alcohol—certainly nobody who had done it voluntarily. It was like this "thing" that I had heard about, but I had a hard time wrapping my head around the fact that people actually did it. I thought something like that only happened after an intervention or when someone was involuntarily committed to a treatment center. You know, the people with the "real" drinking problems. But my dad was living proof that, no matter how much you loved to drink, you could choose to give up alcohol on your own and live to tell about it. It's incredibly impactful to have a real-life example of someone doing something that you think is impossible.

* * *

Todd Kinney

The frequency with which I ran my Race to Nowhere may have gone up and down over the years, but on the whole, I drank the same way at 30 as I did at 20, the same way at 40 as I did at 30. I may not have drunk quite as much as a 30-year-old as I did when I was in college, but the way in which I drank did not change much over time. I almost always had more to drink than others (or certainly wanted to). I almost always got more drunk. I almost always focused more on drinking than anyone or anything else. It was something that was always on my mind. None of those things changed from the time I started drinking until the time I quit.

What did change was my situation and my circumstances. The stakes got higher. My job, marriage, kids. I went from associate in a law firm to partner. From boyfriend to fiancé to husband to dad. Father to babies and toddlers who aren't aware of drinking to father of preteens and teens who are acutely aware of drinking issues. Coming home shitfaced to kids who are thirteen and fourteen is much different from coming home shitfaced to kids who are five and six.

***

When I was a second-year associate at my firm, my working group had a good-bye party at a country club for one of the partners who was leaving to take an in-house job. The party was outside by the pool, with the golf course as the backdrop. It was a perfect summer night, and the open bar made it even better. The entire department was invited, including staff.

It started out innocently enough, with people milling around, making small talk. As the sun went down and the alcohol continued to flow, the crowd thinned a bit. Those who usually had a drink or two left, while those (like me) who were intent on drinking more stuck around and, well, drank more. As these events often do, it gradually evolved (devolved?) from a nice, quiet cocktail party to a rowdier, looser gathering.

Later in the night, two partners got into a debate about who was the better swimmer. To the surprise of no one who is familiar with how foolish the male species can be, they decided to settle the question by jumping into the pool partially clothed to race. I followed suit by jumping in myself. I figured if two partners did it, it was okay for an associate to do it. I kept my pants on, so I guess that counts for something? One other associate got in the pool as well. I stayed in the pool for a few minutes, got out, and drove home shortly after that—in my pants, which were still very wet. When I woke up the next morning, the usual feelings of regret and embarrassment that followed a night of too much drinking were more pointed than usual. I spent most of the day convincing myself that I was overreacting, and that because two partners also had jumped in the pool that made what I had done okay. But that Monday, as I walked from the parking garage into the office, it all came flooding back.

Nobody from work ever said anything to me about that night. I laughed about it with the other associate who'd jumped in the pool—trying my best to disguise the anxiety I felt over the incident. He probably was doing the same. I'm sure there was talk around the office about it. I'm also sure that it didn't reflect well on me. I knew better. I usually was pretty good about keeping things in check at firm events and anything business related (although probably not as good as I thought I was). But I cringe when I think back on that night.

***

In 2005, my best friend got married in Tucson a month before Beth was due with our first baby. I was the best man. Beth was on bed rest at the time because of premature contractions. The doctors didn't think she was in immediate danger of going into labor, but she could be if she didn't take her bed rest seriously. I was a little nervous about traveling to Arizona that close to the due date, especially given her condition. She told me to go and promised to obey her doctor's orders.

Before I left, I wrote down all the return flights in case Beth went into labor and I had to jump on a plane back to Omaha. I kept the list in my wallet (this was in the days before smart phones).

I should have been watching my phone the entire weekend. Instead, the first night there, I got drunk enough that I probably wouldn't even have fielded a call from Beth had she gone into labor—certainly not after I passed out. Nothing would have woken me up then. And if it had, my chances of being able to get my ass to the airport and buy a ticket home in any urgent manner were slim to none. Then if I actually had made my way home, I still would have been drunk or, best-case scenario, hung over. I would have reeked of booze. It would have been quite the scene in the delivery room.

None of that happened that night, luckily. But that's how close I was to fucking up the birth of my first kid—for me and my wife—because I chose alcohol over Beth and my almost-newborn son.

***

In 2013, I had my 20-year high school reunion. I had been to my five-year reunion but not to any of the others. I was really looking forward to this reunion. One of our good friends was going to be back in town, and it seemed like all my other close friends were planning on attending. It was going to be a party.

My group of friends met up at a hotel bar close to where the reunion was taking place. Some of our classmates were there. We hugged, caught up, met each other's spouses. The drinks were flowing. Everyone was happy to see each other. It was fun. I still have a framed picture sitting on my desk at home of me and four of my best friends from that night.

We walked over to the reunion and the fun continued. By now, I had passed the first checkpoint in my Race to Nowhere. While most people would be focused on seeing classmates they hadn't seen in years—you know, the reunion itself—I was focused on continuing my own drinking party. And continue it I did, with gin & tonics. Nothing super embarrassing happened that night at the reunion. I had some conversations that, looking back, the people on the other end were probably happy to get out of. I talked to some classmates who I genuinely wanted to catch up with and have a good conversation with. Instead, because of how drunk I was, I had utterly forgettable conversations with them, totally wasting the opportunity to catch up with people I cared about. We talked about surface-level, superficial stuff, because that's all I could muster. My level of intoxication made it impossible to go any deeper than that. I cringe at how many times this was the case for me.

When the reunion ended, a group of us headed down the street to a different bar. I began to pass out at the table. My buddies had seen this before and were unfazed. We didn't stay long, but I should have been driven home and put into bed at this point. Instead, we ended up back at the hotel—in a room with a couple of my buddies and two women who were in town for the reunion. I knew these women well—we had been friends in high school, and I went to college with one of them. A couple of my friends were planning on staying in the hotel room. The others didn't seem to have any plans to go home anytime soon. Somehow, I was lucid enough to realize that crashing on the floor of a hotel room probably wasn't the best decision, and I started to try to find a way home.

I called an Uber. Then my phone died. The next thing I remember is wandering around downtown Omaha, not really knowing where the hell I was going. I was trying to find the Uber but was walking aimlessly. I ended up in some parts of Omaha that were not safe—especially at 1:00 am. My recollection of this part of the night is limited to small snippets. I still don't know exactly how I got home—it remains somewhat of a mystery to this day.

When I woke up the next morning, I had two distinct feelings. One was relief that I was waking up in my own bed next to my wife instead of in that hotel room. The other was a mixture of disgust, disappointment, fear, and shame for not knowing exactly how I'd gotten home and for having walked aimlessly around downtown Omaha with a phone that had died. That all-too-familiar voice showed up again: "What the fuck are you doing? You're a father of four kids. You're a lawyer. Why are you in this situation again? What's the matter with you? What if you hadn't gotten a ride home last night?" I was back in the parking lot of the Chinese food restaurant staring at my kids in the back seat, three years later, having the same conversation with myself.

I went through all the horrific scenarios that could have played out just as easily. I couldn't believe I had put myself in that position. Yet it was also the least surprising thing in the world.

"Do you want to keep waking up feeling like this?" I asked myself.

The questions lingered this time. I couldn't dismiss them as quickly as I had before, no matter how badly I wanted to.

CHAPTER SEVEN

Let's Talk about Sex

"I'm tired of being the only one who initiates sex," I said. It was a couple of weeks after the reunion. Beth was sitting on our bed, back against the headboard. Her hands were in her lap, and she was slouched over a bit. I was standing at the foot of the bed. She looked down, diverting her eyes to the side—anywhere but at me.

I waited for her to jump in. I'd been having this conversation in my head for months. I wanted her to just read my mind so I would have to say as little as possible.

Silence.

"It seems like such a chore for you. Like an obligation. It's like you're just doing it to get it over with until I start asking for it again. It's getting old."

"I don't know what to tell you. You just want sex more often than I do."

"No, that's not it. I don't care if we have sex more often. I just want you to *want* to have sex every once in a while. That's it! I don't think I'm asking for too much. I don't think you're physically attracted to me."

"I am," she said quietly. She didn't even try to make it sound convincing.

"You say that, but you don't act like it."

More silence. The look on her face was of someone who knew what she needed to say but didn't want to actually say the words.

"Your drinking . . . ," she finally said, still looking away.

"My drinking what?" I blurted out. I knew deep down that I didn't want to go down this road, but my first instinct was to be defensive. My voice was getting louder. Hers was getting softer.

"It's just . . ."

"It's just what?"

More silence.

She still was looking away. I looked at her, waiting for her to answer. The only reason I looked at her was because I was almost certain that she wasn't going to look back at me. Eye contact would mean an end to this dance we were doing.

Then it hit me.

She didn't say the words "I'm not attracted to you because of your drinking," but she didn't have to. Her sad, resigned face, her slouched shoulders, and her avoidant eyes told the story.

We didn't really finish the conversation. Neither of us wanted to. We didn't need to.

The realization cut me to the core. It scared me. Relationships, in my opinion, don't last without physical attraction. Or at least the kind of relationship I wanted didn't last without it. This was not "my husband is annoying me, I need a break from him" stuff. This was fundamental, seismic, turning-point-type of stuff. For a brief moment, I contemplated whether this was even fixable.

When Beth told me without telling me that my drinking was affecting how attracted she was to me, I already was starting to realize that my drinking was causing an issue in my marriage. She never had given me an ultimatum. She never had told me that I should consider quitting. In fact, she told me more than once that she didn't think I needed to actually *quit*. I just needed to figure out how to stop getting so drunk. I needed to learn to drink like a normal person. That was music to my ears. I was so relieved every time she said that. In hindsight, it kept me stuck for a long time.

By 2013, we had been married for eleven years. Our day-after routine was well established by then. I would begin the feeling-out process as soon as I could. It usually didn't take long to figure out whether she was pissed about the night before, and, if so, what level of pissed she was. More often than not, we didn't actually talk about the night before. When we did, it would go something like this:

Me: "I don't know what happened last night."
I would throw in whatever excuse I could muster:

1) Hadn't eaten much.
2) So and so bought me too many drinks.
3) Started drinking too early.
4) The IPAs were stronger than I thought.
5) Gin & tonics got me again.

None of them was ever THE reason. But it didn't stop me from trying. She would look at me with exasperation, like I had three heads.

"I don't understand. One minute you were fine and the next you could barely talk. Can you seriously not control your drinking better than that? You're a grown-ass adult. Why can't you just drink like a normal person?"

"I don't know! Believe me, I wish I could." I so, so desperately wanted to drink like a normal person.

On mornings when we didn't talk about it, I knew what she was thinking. It wasn't much different than what I was thinking myself. She would give me the cold shoulder. I would walk on eggshells until she started to thaw, all the while beating myself up and wallowing in a pile of shame and regret. Eventually she would thaw, I would breathe a sigh of relief and promise myself it wouldn't happen again, and we would all go on about our business.

By 2013, though, the drill was getting old. Despite countless promises to myself that it wouldn't happen again, it kept happening again. Despite me desperately wanting it to never happen again, it kept happening again. There would be times when I would go for months with my drinking in check. But it never lasted for good. Never. The *when* or *how often* wasn't even that important. It was the fact that it *always* happened again. Sometimes I knew it was going to, sometimes it happened without warning. It was as certain as the sun coming up—it always would come back at some point. I was like a cheating spouse who kept getting caught and kept swearing that it was the last time.

This puzzled me, while at the same time it was the least surprising thing ever. It puzzled me because I wanted so badly to just drink like a normal person. Was that too much to ask?! That doesn't sound very difficult on paper. Yet it wasn't surprising because, by this time, I had enough historical data in the bank that only a fool would think it would just magically stop one day. It seems so simple and logical looking back now: the same thing kept happening even though I desperately didn't want it to and hated myself when it did. That's called addiction, or alcohol use disorder, or an unhealthy relationship with alcohol. You can label it whatever you want. The bottom line was, it was a problem that needed to be addressed.

This kind of thing chips away at a marriage. It was hard for me to see this happening in real time—especially since I was trying to convince myself that my drinking problem wasn't actually a Problem. But it was eroding our relationship in a couple of different ways. One, it affected my own self-esteem. When you continually promise yourself that you're going to do something yet continually fail at it, that takes a toll. In the moment, it seems like the feelings of shame, regret, and embarrassment last a couple of days and then they're gone. But really, they don't disappear for good, they only retreat. They're waiting in the wings to come back. And when they do come back, they do so a little bit stronger than before. Each time this happened, my self-esteem took a hit. Even if it was only a tiny hit—maybe even unnoticeable—those tiny hits add up over time.

At the same time, Beth was watching all this from the outside. Just as my feelings of shame, regret, and embarrassment ate away at me from the inside, they affected her perception of me as well. I felt like a failure, at least when it came to managing my drinking, and she saw me as one too. Every time I didn't keep my drinking in check, I was bringing tension into our marriage. I had put an obstacle between us, and with each drinking episode that obstacle got a little bit taller. Like the self-esteem chipping away, you don't really notice it in real time. It was like a cancerous tumor that you know on some level is there, but you don't necessarily know that it's getting bigger.

This kind of thing—something that is the source of tension in a relationship that keeps happening over and over—breeds resentment. It can be anything—gambling, cheating, lying, spending money. Mine was drinking. Beth got to the point where she thought, "Are you kidding me? We're really doing this again?" every time it happened. I don't blame her. Hell, I thought the same thing. It made her feel like I didn't care about our marriage enough. If I knew these drinking episodes brought strife into our relationship and I kept having these drinking episodes, why wouldn't she think that? That was starting to drive a wedge between us. It was slowly pulling us apart.

I was worried about where my marriage was headed. The drinking fights—the morning-after drill—were starting to feel like one of those fights you have over and over as a couple. Probably because we did in fact have them over and over! I remember thinking at the time that if, as a couple, you fight over and over about the same thing without ever doing anything about it, you're asking for trouble. Those things just fester. They don't go away on their own. You can't just not tend to a marriage and hope things like that will go away. It doesn't work that way. Exhibit A was my wife telling me without telling me that she wasn't as physically attracted to me because of my drinking. That was a pretty bright warning light staring me right in the face.

You know when you hear stories about friends divorcing because one of them is having or had an affair? And you can't believe it? It seems like it came out of nowhere? Whenever I heard a story like that, my very first instinct, without fail, was to take inventory of my own relationship. I went straight to: "Shit, that could be us. Could that be us? Could that happen to us? Do we need to start counseling tomorrow?" Beth would always laugh that off and tell me I was overreacting. But nobody ever thinks it can happen to them before it happens to them! I was convinced that if you didn't keep a close eye on that stuff—maintenance-type stuff—you'd wake up one day and find out your wife had been unhappy for a year and was fucking someone else. I did not want my wife to start fucking someone else.

CHAPTER EIGHT

First Sabbatical

I wasn't sure what kind of help I needed. I just knew I needed some guidance. For me, that almost always meant talking to someone who knew more about what I was dealing with than I did. So I found a therapist named Deanna—on the internet. While I wouldn't necessarily recommend this method of choosing a therapist, I happened to get really lucky. She turned out to be fantastic. She could have been awful, or just average, but I got lucky. I still see her regularly today.

I didn't walk into Deanna's office for the first time and proclaim that I needed help with my drinking, even though that was so. I didn't think I needed to quit, of course. Things weren't *that* bad. I just needed to modify the way I drank. It finally was time to learn how to drink like a normal person. My impetus at this point was concern for my marriage, and that my wife would start fucking someone else. Sure, I would have loved to change the way I drank just for my own good, but the prompt that got me there was concern about where my marriage was headed, punctuated by Beth telling me (without telling me) that she wasn't as attracted to me because of my drinking.

The first thing I noticed about my therapist's office wasn't the small painting on the wall, or the two chairs opposite where she sat, or the small table in between the two chairs. It was that it felt warm and calm. The lights were dim, and there was a small water feature in the corner that created a relaxing setting. I sat down in one of the chairs, about five feet across from where Deanna was sitting. Her smile and eyes were soft and welcoming. She instantly made me feel at ease.

"So, tell me what brings you here," she said.

I had a momentary panic attack when I realized that I hadn't really rehearsed my opening lines. Do I open with the drinking? I can't open with the drinking. I don't even know if my drinking is that big of a problem. Then why are you here? I don't know, why am I here?

I settled on, "Well, I've been fighting with my wife a lot lately." Yeah, that sounded pretty normal. And it wasn't completely untrue. Beth and I had been sniping at each other a lot in the several weeks leading up to my appointment. Actually, more than sniping. We had been full-on fighting as well. We weren't in a great spot. And there was the whole me-always-initiating-sex thing.

The fighting bothered me, but what really alarmed me was how easily I would go into shutdown mode. I went from discussing to fighting to shutting down in about fifteen seconds. I would check out and just stew over whatever we were fighting about. That wasn't like me. I normally wanted and needed to talk things out. But I was settling into this unhealthy pattern, and I didn't know how to stop it. I felt like I couldn't stop it, even though I wanted to. Sometimes we would revisit the topic and resolve it. Sometimes we wouldn't. We were also mean to each other when we fought. Not call-each-other-nasty-names-and-scream mean, but meaner than spouses should be to each other. We didn't treat each other well when we fought. It wasn't a healthy or productive pattern.

I told Deanna I wanted to improve my relationship with Beth. I wanted to stop fighting so much. I wanted us to stop being mean to each other. I wanted to stop shutting down so easily. I wanted more control over my emotions. All this was true. It also left out one very large piece of the puzzle that, even feeling at ease in Deanna's office, I still couldn't say out loud. Deanna, of course, knew there was more there than I was saying out loud. So it wasn't long before we were discussing my drinking.

At that very first meeting, Deana recommended that I take a three-month break from drinking.

"I'm sorry, how long?" I think I muttered.

"Three months."

"Shit," I thought to myself. That's what I thought she said. I shifted uncomfortably in my chair.

"As in, one quarter of an entire year? Ninety days? Holy shit, that's a long time."

She may as well have asked me to run into a burning building. I mean, I was prepared to do something. Even take a break of some duration. Maybe two to three weeks. A month max. A month seemed like a good amount of time, right?

"You need at least three months to actually experience some of the changes you'll feel," she answered.

"Really?" I asked, suspiciously. "It seems like I could get that in a month or so. Maybe even a week!"

I quickly went through all the drinking events over the next three months. Thanksgiving. Christmas. Football games. It was the middle of football season! Holiday parties. New Year's Eve! Bowl games. Traveling. I was panicked. Maybe this therapist thing wasn't such a great idea after all.

What would I say to people? How would I explain this? What would people think? I went through about 75 imaginary conversations in my head. They were all awkward and uncomfortable. They were all conversations I had no desire to have. I had no idea *how* to have them. I felt anxiety rush over me. Deanna's idea kept getting worse and worse the more I thought about it.

"I don't know . . ." I said, trying to hide my sheer panic and buy some time to come up with reasons why this was a bad idea, other than I DON'T WANT TO DO THIS.

"You're not agreeing to quit forever. You're just taking a break. Drinking will still be there at the end of the three months," she said.

I let that sit for a moment. Damn it, that was all true. I had never looked at it that way. I didn't *want* to look at it that way.

"Will you agree to at least consider it?" she asked at the end of the session.

"Yes" I replied. I really was going to think about it, I told myself. Well, maybe.

I walked out of her office, through the lobby, and onto the elevator back down to the first floor. I felt like a little kid walking to the edge of the high dive. With every step closer to the edge, I realized I needed to jump, and I got a little more scared at the same time. I had an intense back-and-forth going on inside my head.

"You know you need to do this. Stop running from it."

"Stop being dramatic. You take everything to extremes. You don't need to quit for three months. You just need to make some adjustments."

"You've tried the adjustments. How is that working out for you?"

"Oh, shut the fuck up. Have you tried *everything*? And besides, do you really want to be that guy? Enjoy getting made fun of for the next three months."

"Do you want things to change or not? Do you want to ever stop feeling shitty about your drinking? Stop talking yourself out of this and do the hard thing. You're not giving up drinking forever. You know what you need to do."

So, I jumped off the high dive. My appointment was on a Tuesday. I hadn't drunk since the previous weekend. I figured I already had a couple days in the bank. Might as well get a head start. Looking back, I'm so thankful I had the intuition and courage to give into what I knew I needed to do.

The physical part of not drinking was not all that difficult during my first three-month break. I didn't have a lot of physical cravings that left me dying to pick up a drink. There were plenty of awkward moments that felt weird and uncomfortable. But it wasn't like I was getting the shakes from not drinking. I can be a very motivated person when I set out to achieve a goal. At this point, my goal was three months. I didn't have to worry about forever—just three months. I wanted to prove to myself that I could do it. I was going to accomplish that goal come hell or high water. That desire to reach a goal took me a long way. It gave me the actual willpower to get through a night without giving in. I knew I would feel like a giant failure if I gave in. For that three-month period, I wanted to avoid that feeling more than I wanted a drink. While sheer willpower and "want to" aren't enough for long-term sobriety, it powered me most of the way for that three months.

I learned a lot during those three months. For the first time, I discovered that I drank differently than most people. I never had paid attention to this before. For one, I drank faster than everyone else. I never spent much time observing others' drinking habits, and when I did it was only in relation to mine. I was too focused on my own drinking to notice what other people were doing. What I didn't realize until I was in social situations without a drink in front of me was how long it seemed to take most people to finish their drinks. I almost felt like saying something. "Don't you want to hurry up and finish that? Why is it taking so long?!" I couldn't understand how people didn't drink at the pace I was used to—apparently they all weren't running the Race to Nowhere like I was. I've since found that I drink fast even when I'm not drinking alcohol. It's true with coffee and water.

I also realized how common it was for most people to have one or two drinks with dinner and be done for the night. For me, dinner was sandwiched between a couple drinks at home and postdinner drinks. One or two drinks with dinner and nothing else would be a slow night—one of those "wasted" nights I talked about earlier. Whenever I walked into a restaurant, I felt the need to hurry up and order a drink. The first place my eyes would go to is the bar, as I surveyed where the opening was for me to place that order as soon as possible. I did all this while pretending that I was not in a hurry, that it wasn't a big deal whether we ordered a drink right away. I discovered that not everyone has the goal to get a good buzz on during a night out. Who knew that not everyone is out to get shitfaced? I just kind of assumed that they were, partly because that's what I wanted to believe and partly because I never paid close enough attention to realize it wasn't true. I never had taken the time to realize any of these things, but when you're not drinking, these discoveries smack you in the face. When you're the most buzzed one around—always—it's hard to notice what's going on around you.

One of the reasons why an extended break from drinking can be so helpful is because, at some point, it's inevitable that you'll have an experience that will make you sit back and reflect. I had one of those a couple weeks into my three-month break. It was the Iowa–Nebraska game in Lincoln. Iowa hadn't beaten Nebraska since that 1981 game. They had just started playing each other on a regular basis two years prior, when Nebraska joined the Big 10 Conference. Nebraska won both of those games. The teams were pretty evenly matched going into the 2013 game, but for Iowa fans it still felt like beating Nebraska was this milestone that hadn't been conquered.

I went to the game with Landon (seven at the time) and my dad. Iowa won 38–17, and for us Iowa fans living in Nebraska, this was a big deal. To watch Iowa run away with the game on Nebraska's home field was something special. Landon and I cheered together, hugged, high-fived each other. I have a picture of him and me from that game that I still cherish. Knowing how much that game meant to my dad made it even sweeter. And having him there added to it all. I was walking on air after that game.

Normally, the rest of that day and night would've involved a *lot* of drinking. All the ingredients were there for an epic night of drinking: it was the Friday after Thanksgiving, a holiday weekend, after a huge Iowa win, and I had no real responsibilities the next day other than to lie around and watch more football. The celebration would have been on starting the minute the game ended, and it would have ended with me passing out.

Instead, I was able to drive home from Lincoln and enjoy the rest of the day at home without being obsessed with keeping the party going. I woke up the next day feeling refreshed. But more importantly, I had no regrets from the night before, so there was nothing to taint a truly memorable day with one of my kids and my dad. That was the best part—I had one of those wonderful days with family that *stayed* a wonderful day. It didn't turn into something that made me cringe when I looked back. My drinking didn't ruin it.

Sure, it felt weird not to drink after such a big win, and part of me wanted to drink. I had drunk after big Iowa wins for probably 20 years. But when I woke up the next morning, I *loved* the way I felt. I loved the way life felt. I thought, "Okay, there may be something to this not-drinking thing." It was such a positive, impactful experience that I could look back on later and draw upon. Years later when I was contemplating quitting for good, it was there as a positive experience that made the idea a little less overwhelming.

When the end of the three-month sabbatical came, I felt accomplished. I was proud of myself for reaching my goal. I had learned some things, and I felt much more enlightened about my drinking habits. With this new knowledge and insight, I was ready to get back on the drinking train. But not the same exact train. I really, really loved the lack of hangovers. Going three months without one made me never, ever want to have one again. I once had gone two straight days without eating because I was so hung over. Countless times I'd slept the day away just to feel normal enough to function. Even more often than that, I mindlessly trudged through life's activities with a headache and an upset stomach. Why would you ever do something to yourself that had the potential to make you feel like a hangover did? I wanted to keep drinking, but I really had no desire to ever get drunk again. My new year's resolution that year was to change the way I drank. Continue drinking, but not get drunk. Sounds simple enough, doesn't it?

CHAPTER NINE

In Control

In February 2014, I set out on my new drinking path. The end of my sabbatical happened to coincide with a trip to Champaign, IL, that I had planned with some buddies. We were going for the Iowa–Illinois basketball game. On the one hand, I was glad to be making this trip after my drinking break was over, because it seemed like it would be a difficult trip to make without drinking. On the other hand, it was almost too much right out of the gate. A guys' trip for a sporting event? Talk about jumping back into the deep end of the pool without a life jacket.

I flew to Chicago to meet my buddies before the drive to Champaign. After spending approximately fifteen hours contemplating it, I did not have a drink at the airport or on the plane. My inner dialogue went something like this:

> "Come on, what's one beer at the airport going to do? You're really going to do this from now on? Even though one beer won't get you drunk, you're still not going to have one? Why don't you just order a beer if you want one? It's one beer. What's the big deal? One here and one on the plane will be fine. You'll be completely sober by the time you get to Todd's

house. This is stupid. You're an adult. Have a beer if you feel like having a beer."

At the time, I was really committed to my "new" way of drinking and, deep inside, I feared that if I had a drink either at the airport, or on the plane, or both (i.e., exactly what I would've done under my "old" way of drinking), then nothing would change. After all, if I was going to change things, I needed to change things. I needed evidence that my new way of drinking was taking hold. So I stuck to my guns and didn't have a beer at the airport or on the plane. I decided that waiting until we went to the bar before the game would be appropriate under my new drinking guidelines. That way, I could have a couple drinks, then we would go to the game (where they didn't serve alcohol), and my buzz would wear off in time to drink some more after the game.

And that's what we did. I still remember that first IPA I had at the bar before the basketball game. It tasted soooo good. I had to try really hard not to drink it all in two gulps! I thought about that beer the entire ride from Chicago to Champaign, while doing my best to pretend I wasn't thinking about that beer the entire ride from Chicago to Champaign.

All in all, it was an uneventful night. Iowa won the game, and we had a pretty typical night out. Still, the next morning, I couldn't shake a nagging feeling. Nothing bad had happened. I don't think I drank more than the others I was with. I don't think any of my buddies gave a second thought about my drinking. But there were still parts of the night that were a little sketchy. I remembered walking back to the hotel, but there were bits and pieces after that which I didn't completely remember. Not large sections of time, just not a completely clear memory of the night before.

I convinced myself that the night had gone fine. And it did, for the most part. But part of me thought, "Damn, your first night back at it, and you couldn't hold it together just a little better? Your FIRST night back?" It made me feel a little like a failure—and that pissed me off. Again, nobody on the outside probably noticed a thing. But I knew. That's what mattered.

In my presabbatical days, I wouldn't even have entertained any thoughts that a night like that wasn't a complete success. I would have been patting myself on the back for a job well done, for keeping things under control. But postsabbatical, the bar was higher and my objectives were different. I had more of a truth from which I couldn't run. Over the next few years, this new truth would become a bigger and bigger shadow, something that was annoying and scary but also something that helped lead me down a path of freedom and happiness that I didn't know existed. It started as just a nudge here and there, but eventually it became a push with such force behind it that there was no way to turn back.

I should have paid more attention to those nagging feelings at the time. I should have examined them more, given them more thought. But I refused to dwell on them. "The night was fine, stop obsessing over it," I told myself. So I pushed the thoughts down. Instead, I told myself that the night had been a success. No passing out, no getting way more drunk than everyone else, no embarrassing stories, nothing to regret. That should absolutely constitute a success for my new drinking life—right?

My therapist often would say to me, "You need to figure out *why* you drink." I thought it was an odd question. I never had given that much thought, and when she would ask, I never had a good answer. I didn't really know why. "Because it's fun!" was the most I could come up with. I just liked drinking. I looked forward to it. It made me happy. (Temporarily, at least. Often I just ignored the negatives.) It was just something I liked to do. I've since come to realize that there was more to it than that. There always is.

As a lawyer, everything that comes across my desk does so because something has gone wrong. The shit has hit the fan. It can leave you thinking that anything that can go wrong, will go wrong. So I constantly approach things in life thinking:

1) What are the possible ways in which this can go wrong?

2) How can I prepare for those things happening?

It's a constant loop of trying to prepare for the worst-case scenarios. I'm paid to spot risk, analyze it, and do whatever is possible to mitigate it. That's literally my job: to protect people from things going wrong, and make sure they're in the best possible position for when they do go wrong. Or pull them out of whatever situation they're in because things have gone wrong.

Doing this every day for work naturally spills over into my life. My wife will vouch for that. It can be exhausting living with someone who is constantly wondering what will go wrong and taking steps to mitigate any damage. Some of it is a good thing, but it can take its toll. It can be tiring, for me and for those around me. I've come to realize that drinking was a way to let that go. It was a way to just say, "Fuck it, I'm not worrying about all that stuff for the next four hours." It was a way to numb the reflex to think about what could go wrong and how to prepare for it. It was a break from all that weight.

Drinking was also about control for me, which is ironic because so much of my drinking was underlined by a feeling that, at the end of the day, I couldn't control it to the extent I wanted to. But there's some control in getting to decide when to say "Fuck it." When you get to check out. When you get to numb yourself. When you get to push the real feelings to the side because they feel like too much. Alcohol, and the way I used it (the way a lot of us use it), was a way to control the heavy stuff that came into my life. Or at least to control how and when I dealt with it. That was so appealing to me, as someone who likes to control things as much as possible and who thrives on predictability and order. Of course, all this is just temporary "control," and really just a mirage, but I didn't realize that at the time.

At the end of the day, drinking was a coping mechanism for me. Whether you're a lawyer, teacher, police officer, or stay-at-home parent, everyone wants to find ways to cope with life. Drinking is sold to us as THE way to do that. It's relaxing! You deserve it! This will make you feel better! We're bombarded with these messages 24/7. But alcohol does none of that. Sure, there's some temporary relief. But in the end, it's just an illusion. Alcohol actually makes the anxiety, stressors, and burdens worse. William Porter explains it well in his book, *Alcohol Explained*:

> Essentially, alcohol provides us with a feeling of relaxation. However, the brain and nervous system reacts to this by releasing stimulants and becoming more sensitive, with the result that when the alcohol wears off we are more anxious and unrelaxed than we were before we took the drink. So we are inclined to take another drink, and the relaxing effect of

every drink we take registers on the subconscious, but the corresponding feeling of anxiety does not register on the subconscious as being the result of the alcohol, as it is too far apart in time for the subconscious to link the one with the other. So over time the subconscious mind comes to believe that alcohol will relieve anxiety, so that whenever we suffer anxiety or stress in our lives we encounter a subconscious trigger to take a drink. This in turn can set off the spiral of craving, which means we simply cannot function or enjoy ourselves without a drink. All the while and throughout this entire process, as the body and brain become increasingly proficient at countering the alcohol, the mental relaxation is increasingly outstripped by the physical intoxication, meaning we are increasingly inclined to lose control when we are drinking and end up totally intoxicated. [1]

This is why we so often have anxiety the morning after a night of drinking. I always thought that this feeling was just something in my head. I was disappointed in myself, so I felt the weight of that the next morning. But it's more than that—there's an actual physiological explanation for it. It's a real thing. They call it *hangxiety*. It's why they say alcohol is like pouring gasoline on your anxiety fire. We think it will make things better, and it does for a short time, but then it actually makes our anxiety worse.

As William Porter explains further:

> To put it another way, everyone knows that the more we drink, the more we build up a tolerance to the alcohol, and the more we are capable of drinking. . . . If you look at how much you could comfortably handle when you first started drinking compared with the amount you could drink after a few years, I am sure you will see a marked increase. This is pretty standard stuff and in no way controversial, and the same applies to many other things such as smoking, caffeine intake, etc., but how many of us have stopped to consider what has actually changed that allows us to imbibe a larger amount of a particular poison, an amount that would have

I Didn't Believe It Either

left us extremely ill or even dead had we imbibed it in the first instance? It is not, for example, that our liver becomes stronger. The liver is not a muscle that when exercised becomes stronger. In fact, the more we pummel it the weaker it gets. So what does change?

The changes are in fact twofold. Firstly, those parts of our brain and nervous system that are particularly vulnerable to the depressive effects of alcohol become more sensitive so that they can work even when under the influence of the anaesthetizing effects of alcohol. Secondly, the body becomes more proficient at manufacturing and releasing stimulants and stress hormones to counteract the effect of the alcohol. This is a perfectly natural and healthy reaction. It is the human body dealing with and countering the poisonous effects of an external substance so that we can survive it. The stronger and healthier the human, the more proficiently their body will counter the poisonous effects of the alcohol in this way.

It is also the case that the more often we imbibe alcohol and the greater the quantity we imbibe, the better and more efficient our bodies become over time at countering it. However, perfectly natural and healthy though it may be, the fact of the matter is that when we have parts of our brain and nervous system that are more sensitive, and when we have an increased amount of stimulants and stress hormones in our system, we feel not just unrelaxed but usually out-and-out nervous and anxious. The more we drink, the more pronounced this feeling of nervousness and worry is when the alcohol wears off, and it is quite usual for it to cause full-blown depression. After all, the alcohol will wear off, but the nervous feeling caused by the increased sensitivity and stimulants will remain for some time after.

There are numerous studies dealing with these two effects; however, for practical purposes, the science behind this is neither here nor there. All we need to know is that the

67

relaxing effect of a drink is soon replaced by a corresponding feeling of anxiety. One drink will produce a relatively minor feeling of relaxation and a correspondingly minor feeling of anxiety. However, if we continue larger quantities then the feeling of anxiety is correspondingly increased and can evolve from anxiety into out-and-out depression. [2]

The idea that alcohol helps with anxiety or helps us cope with life is a fallacy. Life isn't easier or more enjoyable with alcohol. We think it is because alcohol lies to us. Most addictive substances do. If the science isn't clear enough for you, the evidence is always there in our own lives, if we're willing to be honest—*really honest*—in our evaluation. It was for me anyway. I just couldn't see it for a long time.

***

In 2013 and 2014, I experienced loss in my life that I had never experienced before. In the span of sixteen months, I lost two people very close to me and our family. One was my sister-in-law, Wendy, who died at age 34 after a courageous battle with cancer. The other was my godfather, Tim Sullivan, whom I had known since birth. He died of Parkinson's at age 66.

We traveled to Denver a couple days before Tim died to say our goodbyes. He had been moved to a hospice facility. The day he died, we took turns saying goodbye. When I was done, I left the room through the back door, which led outside to a courtyard. Tim's three daughters and his wife then went in to spend their final moments with him. I cried as I sat on a green, wrought-iron bench not far from Tim's room. I looked around at the nice landscaping that lined the walking trails in the courtyard. I felt like the setting should make me feel better, but it didn't. After some time, which could have been anywhere from five minutes to an hour, I heard the girls' cries when Tim took his last breath.

My crying turned to sobbing. Body-moving, uncontrollable, exhausting sobbing. I physically ached in a way I did not know was possible. I felt like I might throw up. The grief, sadness, and gut-wrenching finality of it all suffocated me. I stood up to walk to another part of the courtyard, hoping that would somehow, in some way, alleviate what I was feeling, if only a little bit. I was begging for some relief from this overwhelming sadness and despair. Eventually it came, but only after I experienced ache and sorrow that I had not known in my life up to that point. That pain left a mark.

As I reflected on Tim's death in the days and months that followed, the realization that I could do nothing about the pain was startling. How could this be? Tim had had Parkinson's for several years; he died in hospice; we knew for a while that the end was coming. Wendy too—she had ridden a roller-coaster ride with the cancer. She beat it, it came back, she got better, there was hope, and then things got bad again. For her last six months or so, we knew the end was coming. Surely I was doing something during all that time to prepare for the ultimate end, because that's what I did in my life—I prepared for bad things so they wouldn't be quite as bad.

And then the end came for Wendy, and my "preparation" (whatever the hell it even was) turned out to be useless again. That bring-you-to-your-knees pain flooded back, compounded this time by watching my brother sob inconsolably in my mom's arms, and by thinking about their two young boys who had just lost their mother at age 34. Wendy died in the middle of the night. By the time the sun came up, I felt like I hadn't slept in a week.

There was no way to prepare for either of these events. There was no way to control, minimize, or regulate the excruciating hurt that came with them. Death doesn't work like that. Life doesn't work like that.

You might think this realization that I couldn't control everything would prompt me to question my unending, desperate quest to control my drinking. However, thinking that would mean vastly underestimating how much I wanted to keep drinking. I was still very much convinced that I could, in fact, control my drinking. I was even more confident of this fact now that I was armed with all the knowledge gained from my three-month break. Even with the life-changing discovery that Tim and Wendy's deaths forced on me—that control is just an illusion—and even with ample evidence that controlling my drinking just wasn't attainable, I doubled down on controlling my drinking. What could go wrong?

CHAPTER TEN

The Moderation Game Continues

The next couple of years were fine from a drinking standpoint . . . 75% of the time. I developed some other moderation hacks that I used on a regular basis. One of them was a list I made of how drinking too much made me feel. I kept it on my phone. I still have it today. This is the list:

Shame
Embarrassed
Regretful
Want to go back and change it
Lack of respect from others
Lack of self-respect
Not worth it
Feel so much better the next day (when I don't overdo it)
Relationship problems
Feel like a bad father
Irresponsible

I would look at the list before a night out, when I was preparing myself to keep things under control. Sometimes I would look at it during a night out. On almost every occasion when I drank more than I wanted to, there was a point I could go back to later and say, "Yep, that's when it flipped. That's when things went from a normal night out to a night where I drank too much." When I felt that moment coming on, sometimes I would pull the list out and read it. It always grabbed my attention and pulled me back on track for a normal night. The problem was, there were nights when I just didn't want to look at the list. So I didn't.

At the time, I thought of the list as an effective moderation tool, which it was—when I chose to use it. Looking back on it now, I think of the list differently. Now I think, "If you do something that makes you feel all those things, why wouldn't you just give it up completely?" Is there anything else in life besides alcohol that could make us feel those things, and instead of just giving it up we would try to figure out a way to make it work? If a certain food made us feel all those things, would we try to moderate the intake of that food? If a medication made us feel those things, would we even entertain the idea of continuing to take the medication? If a friend came to you and said, "Often when I eat broccoli, I wake up the next day feeling regretful and embarrassed, I don't like myself, and sometimes I throw up," what would you tell that friend? Would you tell him to keep eating broccoli, just find a different way to do it? The logical response, surely, is, "Stop eating broccoli." Of course, by merely moderating, I thought I was "fixing" those things and making sure they wouldn't happen again. It took a while before I came to the realization that moderating those things wouldn't "fix" them or prevent me from feeling those reactions. Moderating my drinking might make the consequences less frequent, but it wouldn't end them altogether.

I also would preplan breaks in my drinking. Most often I would do this when I knew I would be drinking over a longer period. My wife and I took a couples' trip to Chicago to celebrate a friend's birthday. It was during football season, so Saturday naturally involved a long day of barhopping and football watching for the guys. I knew that day would be a challenge and that, if I didn't put some sort of plan in place, it would not end well. So I decided I would take a 1.5-hour break in the middle of the afternoon. (One hour seemed not quite long enough, but two hours seemed a little too daunting, so an hour and a half seemed like a nice compromise.) When my break time hit, I actually left the bar, walked around the block to Starbucks, ordered an iced coffee, and walked around for a bit. The day (and night) of drinking continued, but I was able to keep it under control. The day ended with a midnight cheeseburger from room service as I watched some West Coast football game. Midnight cheeseburger aside, the day/night was a success because:

1) I remembered going to bed,
2) My wife went to bed before me,
3) I hadn't done anything embarrassing or regrettable.

A different version of the "taking breaks" hack was simply waiting until later in the night to *start* drinking. My wife's birthday is on New Year's Eve. In 2014, she turned 40, and we had a big party for her at our house. I spent a *lot* of time thinking about how to keep my drinking under control that night. I knew this party was a big deal for her. I was determined not to let my drinking mar the night in any way. I knew that feeling all too well, and the last thing I wanted was to scar her big birthday party with yet another episode of me drinking too much. In hindsight, the amount of time, thought, and energy I put into keeping my drinking under control should have told me everything I needed to know.

After much deliberation, I decided that I would not start drinking until 10:00 that night. That was later than I wanted to wait, but I didn't want to take any chances. I knew myself too well, and anything before 10:00 was a risk.

I had a lot of duties as host that kept me busy and made it easier to spend the first part of the night not drinking. I was making sure the food and bar were in good shape, greeting people, checking in on people's drinks, trying to talk to everyone, and taking the trash out. It's amazing what a good host you can be when you're sober. But man, I was watching the clock like a hawk. When we were little, my sister and I gave up candy for Lent one year. The day Lent was over, noon was magic hour, when we could officially have candy again (don't ask me why it was noon). My sister and I put two chairs in front of the microwave clock and sat there staring at it for several minutes waiting for it to hit 12:00, so we could scarf down as much candy as our parents would let us. That's how I felt that night, waiting for 10:00 to roll around. Once it did, I didn't waste much time catching up to everyone. I got plenty drunk, but, all things considered, the night was a success. I kept it under control, my wife had a great time, and there were no regrets the next morning. I was immensely proud of myself the next day.

***

In the fall of 2016, our entire family went to Iowa City for Iowa's opening football game. It was late by the time we got to town, so we put the kids to bed shortly after we got to the hotel. It wasn't late enough for me to go to bed though, so I ventured out by myself to my favorite dive bar, which was about a five-minute walk from our hotel. I grabbed a seat at the bar and was in heaven. I was in my favorite town on earth, on the eve of the college football season, sitting at my favorite bar, drinking really good beer. I don't remember how many I had, but it was enough that I was getting to that really good buzz. It was the moment when most people automatically take a break or stop because they're starting to feel drunk. For me, it was the moment that usually made it impossible to slow down. Where the next drink was almost irresistible. It was that point when the bartender asks whether you want another, and you do a split-second justification in your head why it's okay to have another, even though deep down you know that a "normal" drinker wouldn't order one. So, naturally, I ordered another beer.

But this time, I took one sip—and changed my mind. I beat back the urge to have one more. Instead, I got up from my stool, left the full beer sitting there, walked out of the bar, and went back to the hotel where my family was sleeping. It was like common sense smacked me in the face the moment that last beer was put in front of me. I was quite proud of myself, and I spent the entire walk back to the hotel patting myself on the back for my huge victory.

"Look at how I've matured! Look at me walking away from a full beer because I don't need it! I *really have* changed the way I drink! This is how a normal person drinks!" The accolades were flying. Never mind that I had left my family sleeping in a hotel room to go drink at a bar by myself.

***

All these moderation tools were very effective—when I used them. They forced me to look up from my Race to Nowhere. They slowed things down for me. It was almost as if I needed confirmation that I could take a break from the race and would survive. "See, you won't die if you have to wait more than three minutes in between drinks." It was like I was discovering that reality for the first time. When I employed these tactics, I never had a night I regretted.

Another moderation hack I imposed was to put a limit on the number of drinks I would have. This was much less successful. I rarely stuck to the predetermined number. I was constantly negotiating with myself to raise the number. I could come up with any excuse in the book to do that, such as the following:

- That drink wasn't very strong.
- That beer wasn't very good, so it doesn't count against my number.
- We're staying out later than I thought.
- So-and-so just ordered another drink.
- Someone else is driving home.
- So-and-so is really drunk; I can have another and still not be as drunk as him.
- I've made it this long and I'm not that drunk.
- I don't have to get up tomorrow for anything—don't waste this opportunity.

Or I would simply stop counting. The self-imposed limit would go out the window "just because."

When I did stick to the predetermined number, I always felt good about my night out the next morning. But in the moment, there was so much push and pull.

"Do you want another drink?"

"Yes, I would like another drink."

"Well then, have another one. What harm is one more drink going to do?"

"Don't have another one. You put a limit on the number for a reason. You know how this goes."

"It will be fine."

"No it won't."

"But we're going to be here for two more hours. How am I going to stay here and socialize for another two hours without another drink?"

"You'll figure it out—stick to your plan."

"Fuck your plan. This is stupid."

This internal debate just played on a loop inside my head. The exact conversation might change slightly, but it was always the same general idea. Constant negotiating. Relentless rationalizing. Constant pep talks. It was nonstop. It was exhausting. Even when moderating was successful, it was So. Much. Work. There's a reason for the saying, "If you want to find out if you have a drinking problem, try moderating."

* * *

In the fall of 2018, I felt my drinking getting loose again. I was settling into old patterns. It was like all the lessons I had learned from my initial three-month sabbatical were wearing off. I figured it was a good sign that I was aware of this—another indication that I had, indeed, changed the way I drank. But I knew I needed to do something. I needed a reset. I decided to take another three-month break.

This time, I wasn't quite as rigid as with the first sabbatical. During the first break, I didn't have a sip of alcohol. I made no exceptions. This time, I drank twice during the three months. Once was after my best friend's dad died. My friend had come back to town for the funeral, and I was meeting him at his mom's house to see him and his mom. He was not aware that I was taking a break, and he asked me to bring some beer to his house so we could talk about his dad over a beer. I did have one beer, but I left the rest at his mom's place.

The other time I drank was at an Iowa tailgate with one of my good friends from Chicago. We have season tickets together. We met in Iowa City with our sons to go to a game. It seemed weird to not be drinking, and I felt it would impact my buddy's enjoyment of the day. I knew that if the roles were reversed, I would feel somewhat self-conscious about drinking by myself (and when I say "self-conscious" what I really mean is, I would be worried that I couldn't drink as much as I wanted to because it would be more noticeable if I was the only one drinking). He didn't really feel like that, of course, but I projected that onto him as a rationale for me to have a couple of drinks during my sabbatical. The tailgate was pretty low-key. I think I had three beers the whole day.

After the game, we hung out at the tailgate for a while, then eventually made our way back to the hotel. When we got there, we ran into a guy we know who has season tickets right behind us. It was late and we were all ready to turn in for the night. But the guy bought me a beer. However, while I took it up to the hotel room, I didn't drink it. I left it sitting on the counter all night. Another big victory! Yet more evidence that I had things under control, and that I had made real changes to the way I drank. I patted myself on the back again, just like I had on the walk back to the hotel where my family was sleeping.

Those of us with drinking issues, we tell ourselves all sorts of lies about our drinking:

- I don't drink *that* much.

- I wasn't *that* bad last night.

- I don't have a problem because I drink less than so-and-so.

- I had to drink because so-and-so was there.

- I need a drink to get through this.

- I could quit if I wanted to.

- I didn't want to drink, but someone bought me one.

- I'll drink tonight and then take some time off.

- I'm going to keep it under control tonight. I'm moderating successfully.

We're constantly justifying things around our drinking to facilitate our drinking and make ourselves feel better about it. But at the end of the day, they're all lies. Almost *everything* we tell ourselves about our drinking is a lie. Because if we were dead honest with ourselves, that would mean we had a problem. If we dug into our drinking and why we drink and what we think might happen if we stopped, there would be a whole new set of issues to examine. We might be confronted with the idea of needing to do something about our drinking. And that's scary as hell, and a whole bunch of other things.

This sabbatical felt different from the first one. I was trying to put a band-aid on a problem that required something more. I still was selling myself on the same lies, but having a bit more trouble doing so. I didn't have a complete grasp on what was going on, but I knew that *something* was afoot. I thought I had things under control (fixed) after my first sabbatical. Now I was being confronted with the frightening possibility that I had not, in fact, changed the way I drank. My issues with alcohol—the ones that had been there nearly since Day One—hadn't gone away after all. Shit, shit, shit. What if this moderation thing wasn't working after all? The mere thought made me anxious. I wanted to turn and run whenever these thoughts popped into my head. I was scared to death, because if I was wrong about fixing things, what was left to do other than quit? But wait a minute, didn't the fact that I had (voluntarily!) imposed another sabbatical on myself mean that I was in a different category from those who had a *real* problem? Wasn't I different from those who *needed* to give up alcohol *completely*? People who need to quit don't address their issues with sabbaticals, right? That side of my inner debate won out. Again. But the margin of victory was smaller this time.

CHAPTER ELEVEN

Nonalcoholic

A round this time (the winter of 2018), my kids started making comments about everyone's drinking, including mine. They would ask, half joking but not really, "Are you guys going to get drunk tonight?" Or they would make comments about "the parents" drinking too much. Kids just don't blurt these things out mindlessly. They do it because their parents' drinking is on their minds. They don't know how to fully process or deal with their feelings about adults drinking. I think it scares them and makes them uneasy, like it did to me when I was a kid. It makes them feel less than safe. One of the ways they deal with that is through "funny" comments or jokes. But deep down, I think it really affects them. Safety is so important to kids. They need and want a safe, comfortable space so badly. We take that away from them when we drink too much. There's not a parent in the world who wants to do something that makes their child feel less than 100% safe, but we do it all the time when we drink.

In June 2019, my friend Charles and I took some of our kids and their friends to a College World Series game. The CWS is Omaha's showcase event. I grew up going to CWS games with my family, and now I take my kids every year. My parents have had tickets for years. It's always a fun time in Omaha. The city really embraces the event. There is plenty of partying to do if you're looking for that, but it's also a nice family event.

I Didn't Believe It Either

This day, we all drove to the game in one car. The area around the stadium is filled with bars and restaurants. We milled around there for a while before heading into the stadium. Somewhat surprisingly, there was not a lot of drinking before the game. Charles usually was ready to hit it hard, but the difference was fine with me, since I was driving. Once we all got inside the stadium, we split up because our seats weren't together. I sat with Charles. Two of the older kids sat together in one section, and the younger kids sat together in another section. I didn't drink much: three beers over a four-hour period. When it came time to meet up inside the stadium to walk to the car, Austin walked up to me and said, with a slight smile on his face, "Dad, do we need to take an Uber home?" I thought this was an odd question, since I wasn't drunk, and Charles didn't seem particularly drunk either. Austin hadn't seen us down a bunch of beers before the game, so I wasn't sure where he was coming from.

"No, we don't need to take an Uber. Why do you ask that?" I replied.

"Well, sometimes when you and Charles get together, things can get pretty rowdy," he said, with the same slight smile on his face.

I brushed it off as well as I could in the moment. "No, it's fine, buddy. I haven't had very much to drink. I would never put you kids in that position."

The truth was that I had put the kids in that position—more times than I was willing to admit. Not that I had driven them when I was completely trashed, but certainly there'd been times when I was over the legal limit. Even now, it makes me cringe.

I couldn't shake Austin's comment. It nagged at me and weighed on me the rest of the day. I told Beth about it later that night, just to try to get it off my chest. It didn't work. It was the last thing I thought about when I went to bed and the first thing I thought about when I woke up the next morning. Here was my fourteen-year-old son mustering up the courage to ask his dad whether we needed to take an Uber home because I had a habit of drinking too much when I got together with Charles (and, let's be honest, at many other times as well). It's hard for kids to talk about sensitive things like their parents drinking, so for him to bring that up meant it was weighing on him.

This was on the heels of a horrible tragedy in our community. About two weeks prior to our CWS outing, five teenage girls were in an accident involving alcohol after a graduation party. Four of them died. These were good kids who made a terrible mistake and paid the ultimate price. This made an extra impact on me because Austin was approaching driving age, and of course you worry about something like that happening to one of your kids. It was such a harsh reminder of how things can change in an instant and how one bad decision can have dire consequences.

I thought a lot about this crash as I was pondering Austin's comment to me. What was I doing? What kind of dad behaves in a way that causes his kid to worry about having a safe ride home from a baseball game? A parent's most important job is to protect his kids and make them feel safe. I was doing precisely the opposite of that. My behavior was adding anxiety to his life. What kind of parent does that? What the fuck was I doing? The fact that my drinking was causing my son anxiety was a stark realization that was really, really hard to run from. I felt like a bad dad, a bad person. I was back in the Chinese restaurant parking lot. I kept coming back to the same question: Is this the best dad I can be? Is this the dad I *want* to be? It was getting harder and harder to reconcile my drinking reality with the desire to be the best dad I wanted to be for my kids.

Coincidentally, around that same time, while making small talk with opposing counsel after a mediation in Orlando, the other lawyer commented that he had given up drinking when his oldest turned thirteen (Austin was fourteen at the time). He wanted to set a better example for his kids, who were at the age where they recognized when people got drunk. His comment probably seemed inconsequential to him at the time. I nodded in response and said, "Oh wow, good for you," as I tried to suppress the voice inside my head urging me to examine all this more deeply. I didn't appreciate it fully at the time, but this lawyer—someone of a similar age and station in life, with the same job, with kids my kids' ages, telling me he had given up drinking just because he thought it was the right decision—gave me permission to explore the matter more. It was like looking in the mirror and realizing, ever so briefly, that quitting wasn't impossible.

Even though Austin's comment hit me so hard and prompted such self-examination, and despite the lawyer's comment at mediation, I *still* wasn't ready to go "there." Quitting altogether was not on the table yet. But I knew I had to do *something*—Austin's comment was jarring enough that doing nothing was not an option. So, I honed in on the drinking-and-driving aspect. I decided that I would stop drinking altogether whenever I was driving any of the kids anywhere. I figured that would set a good example of what to do when you're driving and when you're around drinking. But even when adults drink responsibly and then drive, do kids really "get" that? Do kids see an adult stop after two beers and think, "Oh, they're okay to drive because they're an adult, adults process alcohol differently, and they stopped before they became legally impaired"? Or do they think, "Okay, Dad drives after two (or three or four) beers and seems fine, so I can have a couple beers and still drive and be okay"? I don't think they make those distinctions. And do we really want to teach them—as teenagers—that drinking and driving is all about knowing when to stop? Or do we want to model what we say all the time, which is, "Don't drink and drive—period"? So I decided to stop drinking altogether, when I was driving with the kids, just to set a better example.

That made me feel sufficiently better in the moment. But like with most of my rules and moderation attempts, I found shortcuts. Our family takes two cars almost everywhere, so whenever we were out and had two cars, I secretly hoped that the kids would ride with Beth, because that meant I didn't have to refrain. They usually preferred to ride with Beth anyway, but I subtly encouraged it. I would breathe a sigh of relief when they ended up with her. Being able to drink outweighed any possibility of quality time in the car with my kids.

Despite my best efforts, this version of a band-aid did little to assuage the weight of Austin's comment. The sting of his innocent yet indicting question was still there. I told myself that I had done something to rectify those feelings of discomfort from making my kid feel unsafe, but really, had I done much? Was I truly making any meaningful change? Was I getting to the root of the problem?

During this time, I did a lot of analysis about whether I was an *alcoholic*. Was it even possible for someone like me to be an alcoholic? I had what probably looked like the perfect life, from the outside. We are a two-lawyer family. We make a very good living. We have four healthy kids. A nice house, nice cars. Country club membership. All the markers of what we tell ourselves constitutes success in today's world. From the outside, it looks pretty good. And it is pretty good, if I'm being honest. I've lived a very blessed, fortunate life.

But what nobody saw was the inner turmoil that was bubbling inside me constantly. The shame and regret that showed up every morning after drinking too much. The push and pull of wanting so badly to drink like a normal person and not understanding why that eluded me too often. The tension with my wife. The nonstop work involved in keeping things under control. The way drinking dominated my thoughts. None of this showed up in Facebook and Instagram posts. I literally thought I was the only person in the world who struggled with my relationship with alcohol in these ways, which only intensified the feelings of shame and desperation.

I knew there were alcoholics, but I had this preconceived notion in my head of what an alcoholic looked like, what he did, how he acted, what his drinking was like. You know, the guy who rolls out of bed, takes a swig from a vodka bottle hidden in the bedside table, and gets on with his day. The guy who shows up to work hammered. The one who shows up to his kids' events drunk or smelling of alcohol, or who doesn't show up to those events at all. The one who stays out until 2 am on weeknights. The one who starts drinking at lunch. The one who goes to the bar more nights than he doesn't. The one who loses jobs because of his drinking. The one who everyone knows has a problem. I knew those people existed—the "real" alcoholics. I didn't know that others like me existed.

Part of that was from what society tells us. Part of it was a subconscious move on my part to avoid confronting my own issues. If I confined my personal definition of people with alcohol issues to the "real" alcoholics, then clearly I didn't fit into that category and didn't need to seriously consider giving it up. On the few occasions that I allowed myself even to contemplate that I might be an alcoholic, I quickly and reliably rebutted that possibility by reminding myself that I voluntarily had given it up for three months at a time—twice! True alcoholics don't do that! They *can't* do that! So there. It was settled. I wasn't an alcoholic. I just "had issues" with alcohol. The furthest I would go was admitting that I didn't have a great relationship with alcohol. While not perfect, that's much different (better!) than being an alcoholic. I had this debate with myself countless times over the years. It always ended with the same conclusion. And it was always bullshit.

I Didn't Believe It Either

From the fall of 2018 to the fall of 2019, I sort of took the guardrails off my drinking. That's not to say that I started drinking all day, every day (I still wasn't drinking on weeknights), but I stopped trying so hard to control it when I did drink. It was just so much damn work, and I was tired of doing it. I needed a break. That meant more nights that I didn't remember how they ended. More occasions when I was the drunkest person in the room. More day drinking. More incidents of having five drinks when everyone else was having two. More cringe-worthy moments. More shame and regret the following morning. More tension with Beth.

During these periods I always felt a little out of control, but, at least for a time, instead of trying to rein it in, I almost embraced the free fall. It was easier to do that than to sit up and take an honest look at what was happening. It was so much less work. No rules, no thinking, no counting drinks, no breaks, none of that bullshit. Just having fun without any of the stupid fucking rules. Sometimes in life we choose the easiest path, even though we know it's not the best one.

Looking back, it's interesting that my drinking got loose at the same time that I was deliberating whether I was a true alcoholic. You'd expect it to go the other way. Something that always accompanied these loose drinking times was the knowledge (even if only on a subconscious level) that the loose period couldn't/wouldn't last forever. I knew that something would shake me back into the work of keeping my drinking under control—often with renewed motivation and the latest hack that was guaranteed to work this time. I used that knowledge to justify not doing something right then and there. It was okay to let the loose period slide for a bit. I'll come back home, I always do. During these times, I'm almost waiting, begging for something bad to happen to jolt me back onto my path.

Nothing pairs quite as perfectly with a loose drinking period as a limo trip with the guys. Every year during football season, some friends and I take a limo from Omaha to Iowa City and back for an Iowa game. One buddy drives up from Kansas City for the trip; another flies in from Chicago; the rest live in Omaha. It's always a great time. There are coolers full of beer and lots of liquor. Some years, depending on the game time, we leave Omaha at 5 am. Regardless of when we leave, the drinking usually starts within 30 minutes of hitting the road. We drink the whole way there, then tailgate for a little while, go to the game, hit our favorite bar after the game, then climb back into the limo, where we drink on the way home (or pass out, or some combination of the two). It's every bit as much of the shit show as you might imagine.

In the fall of 2019, the trip didn't disappoint. The game was at 2:30, which was the sweet spot for not having to leave Omaha too early, yet still having enough time to tailgate after arriving in Iowa City, and then still allowing time for a stop at our favorite bar after the game. I don't remember the tailgating portion of this trip. It wasn't until I saw a picture of us at the tailgate that I even knew it had happened. For some reason still unexplainable today, I spent the majority of the game not in our regular seats but walking around the stadium and standing in various spots to watch portions of the game. If I saw an empty seat, I grabbed it, but most of the time I spent standing. I was able to put only some of these pieces together from the pictures I took throughout the game.

The game itself did not go Iowa's way. When Penn State scored with five minutes left to go up by eleven, I decided I'd seen enough and, in another move that is unexplainable to this day, jogged the entire way to our favorite bar. The bar is a mile from the stadium. I can't prove this, but I recall running at an impressive pace. I remember thinking that the run would help burn off the frustration I was feeling from the game. I'm not sure it worked. All I remember is being out of breath and hot from running in the same winter clothes I'd worn to the game to stay warm. I was sweating by the time I took my seat at the bar.

My phone died shortly after I got to the bar (of course), so I couldn't text my buddies to let them know I was there. Not that it mattered—they knew me well enough not to be too alarmed that I didn't sit with them and was nowhere to be found when the game ended. Nobody was shocked when they arrived to find me already at the bar after making the unusual decision to walk there from the stadium.

One of my friends was nodding off at the bar, which would signal to most people that it was time to leave. For me, it was validation that I wasn't the drunkest one in the group, which permitted me to keep drinking. We left the bar at around 10 pm for the four-hour ride home. I continued to drink for the first half of the ride home, then spent the second half alternately passing out and waking up. I remember pulling into the driveway, but that's about it for memories from the last part of the night. Nothing spectacularly bad happened that night, but as I embarked on my customary analysis the next day of how well I'd kept my drinking in check, I was bothered by two things:

(1) not remembering the tailgate,

(2) wandering the stadium during the game instead of sitting with my friends.

The tailgate bothered me because it had been at 1:00 in the afternoon. How drunk do you have to be to not remember 1:00 in the afternoon? We'd tailgated in the same location as my regular tailgate, which I'd been using for several years. It was a lot of the same people every week, so I knew some of them well from years of Iowa football Saturdays together. Yet I had no recollection of what I may have said to any of them or how I'd acted. I didn't like how that felt.

The wandering bothered me because of something that had happened during our limo trip four years prior. In 2015, I'd pulled a similar stunt. I left my seat near my buddies to wander the stadium—only this time I decided to see whether I could make my way onto the field. I had been on the sidelines for a couple Iowa games a few years before that—legally—and it was really cool. I decided that it was time to do it again—except this time I didn't have the credentials to allow me to be there.

At the end zones of Iowa's stadium, there's no wall between the bleachers and the field itself. If you're sitting in the first row of one of the end zones, your feet are at ground level. If you want to walk out onto the field, all you have to do is stand up and take about ten steps forward, and you'll be standing in the end zone. The only "barrier" is one of those retractable belts that are used in airport security lines. And even those don't extend the entire width of the end zone. The majority of security people around the field are rent-a-cops.

I slowly made my way to the bottom of the student section, where I waited for an opening to saunter onto the field. I looked around and didn't see any security guards, or really any attempt at all to keep people from entering the field area. I took a couple steps away from the last bleacher, inching closer to the field itself, thinking for sure that someone was going to spot me and direct me to turn around, at which time I simply would play dumb and give them a confused "how did I end up here?" look. A foolproof plan, to be sure. Only nobody stopped me. So I kept walking, until I ended up in the corner of Kinnick Stadium, on the Iowa sideline, in front of the cheerleaders and student section. I tried my best to blend in with the other, legally credentialed sideline occupants. I took my phone out and pretended like I was on a call. I couldn't possibly be exposed if I was on a phone call. In my inebriation, the phone call gave me some sort of magic legitimization, as if a security officer who was thinking of interrogating me would see my fake phone call and instantly back off.

I stood on the Iowa sideline for a few minutes, amazed that I was there. My bravado was growing as I realized that this was easier than I'd thought it would be. I decided to make my way over to the Minnesota sideline. This was risky, as I would be leaving the small group of people with whom I had blended in well and exposing myself to a whole new set of eyes that might notice me. There was only one thing to do: take out my phone and begin another fake call.

With the second fake call initiated, I walked the length of the end zone, in front of the student section and behind the uprights, in the ten yards or so between where the end zone ended and the bleachers began. I turned the corner onto the Minnesota sideline, in a similar spot to where I had been standing on the opposite sideline. The highlight was when Iowa's running back ran right by me during a long touchdown run near the end of the game that iced the win for Iowa. Luckily, I was off my fake phone call by then, which allowed me to gesture wildly that the running back needed to keep running that way, toward the end zone—as if he wouldn't know where to go unless I helped him.

After the game was over, I was looking for the best way out of the stadium. Not being used to field access, I wasn't sure how to get out of the stadium from there. I walked up a tunnel that I thought would lead me to the concourse and out of the stadium. Instead, I found myself right around the corner from the visitor's locker room. I could hear the Minnesota players rustling around inside. It was then that I noticed two women sitting on folding chairs guarding the entrance to the locker room. One of them asked whether she could help me. I mumbled something about being lost, turned around, and walked as fast as I could back down the tunnel, and back onto the field, where I found an actual exit.

For the rest of the night, I reveled in my rebellious experience. I bragged about it like a teenage boy who had just snuck out of the house for the first time. The stupidity of what I'd done didn't hit me until the next day. I am an Iowa season-ticket holder. If I had been caught, I easily could have had my season-ticket privileges revoked. I could have been arrested. I could have been charged with a crime. How would I have explained any of that to my kids? I beat myself up over it, had the familiar talk with myself about how I shouldn't be doing those things as a forty-something professional, and vowed—for the 127th time—that it never would happen again. That's why the wandering in 2019, while it didn't include the on-field access, bothered me so much. It felt too close to what had happened in 2015. Another broken promise. Another failure.

My loose drinking in the fall of 2019 also fell during a period of more work travel than usual. Traveling for work always meant more drinking for me. I threw my "no drinking on the weeknights" rule out the window. I was by myself, which meant drinking freedom! I could drink how I wanted without having to worry about someone noticing how much I was drinking. I was so in my own head about my drinking. My wife never counted my drinks or watched them that closely, but I always felt accountable to her and my kids. Sometimes that accountability felt like limitations on my drinking, but when I was by myself on a business trip, I could shed those limitations. If I wanted to have two drinks before dinner, three at dinner, and three more at the bar afterward, then I could. All I had to do was sound sober enough when I called home at night before the kids went to bed. I didn't have to worry about being presentable when I got home to Beth and the kids. This was the best kind of drinking.

The week following the limo trip, I had to go to Washington, DC, to speak at a conference. The trip went very well, the speaking engagement went off without a hitch, and I got some quality time with a client. That, of course, called for a celebration Thursday night, after all the work was out of the way. So naturally I got drunk. I had an early flight to Phoenix the next morning. I was meeting Beth there for a long weekend at a resort, with no kids, to celebrate a good family friend's fortieth birthday. I forgot to set an alarm, but somehow I still managed to get up in time to make it to the airport for an early flight—dragging and hung over. The hangover didn't stop me from ordering a bloody mary at 8 am.

I knew the Arizona weekend was going to be a party. I didn't entertain seriously the idea of committing to "responsible" drinking that weekend. My motivation was already low as a result of my loose drinking the several weeks prior (what's the harm in one more weekend without rules?). The celebratory nature of the weekend, the fact that the group that was going was always a good time, a carefree weekend without kids. . . . All that easily won out over all the work, effort, and discipline that would have been required on my part to keep my drinking in check. I really was looking forward to the weekend, and I wasn't beating myself up for not wanting to do the work to keep my drinking from getting out of control. I was giving myself a pass. Little did I know that that weekend would end up changing my life forever.

CHAPTER TWELVE

Making My Parents Sad

"Your parents are staring at you," my wife whispered into my ear as we sat down for dinner in a private room at the resort.

"What?" I answered with the kind of indignation and dismissiveness that only a sufficiently drunk person can muster.

"Your parents are staring at you," she repeated.

She was trying to get me to go back to our room because, according to her, I was too drunk to eat dinner with our group. In my mind, I was fine. She was overreacting. In reality, my wife did not overreact often, even when it came to my drinking. But she definitely was overreacting this time. She just needed to leave me alone so I could eat dinner. And maybe get another drink.

"Whatever," I thought to myself.

I didn't have time right then to process what Beth was telling me. It was too much to unpack. Too unpleasant. I couldn't let that comment sit with me for longer than a split second, so I didn't. Plus, I was drunk and needed to keep the party going. Anything that got in the way of that had to be tossed aside. That was nonnegotiable. And in that moment, Beth was getting in the way. As was the thought of my parents looking at their oldest child, now a forty-four-year-old adult, as a drunk mess.

Todd Kinney

* * *

The day had started off innocently enough. It was a Saturday, our second day at the resort. The night before, we'd sat around the fire pit having some drinks. It had been a fairly long drinking day, as it often was when we got together with the Sullivans. I've known the Sullivan family my entire life. Tim and Ann, the parents, are my godparents. They have three daughters, Erin, Kerry, and Clare, who are like sisters to me and my siblings. We grew up vacationing together. The Sullivan girls all went to Iowa. They are our second family.

That day I kept my drinking in check, for the most part, although I retired to our room early because I was falling asleep by the fire pit. That counted as "keeping it in check" for me after a long day of drinking at a resort.

On Saturday, Iowa had a football game at 9 am Arizona time. Clare's husband had arranged for the resort to play the Iowa game on the giant screen in the courtyard. So we all met there and watched the game together. It was a nice setup. I'm actually not fun to watch an Iowa game with. I don't like people talking about anything other than the game. I have to strain to keep my emotions in check. I'm loud. I get grouchy if things aren't going well. If Iowa goes three and out on the first possession of the game, I become convinced they're going to lose 42–0.

Somewhat surprisingly, I didn't have a drink during the game. It was a combination of feeling slightly hung over from the night before and trying to pace myself for what I figured would be another long drinking day. Also, it was 9 am local time, which wasn't necessarily a deal breaker, but when you're with your parents, even at forty-four years old, you feel like maybe you should hold off until at least halftime. Well, I managed to hold off the entire game. Yay me!

Iowa won the game, which put me in a good mood and made me want to celebrate. Combine this with the fact that I was patting myself on the back for not drinking during the game, the sun was shining, I didn't have any parental responsibilities to worry about, the pool was calling and, well . . . that's a recipe for things going off the rails.

We spent most of the afternoon at the pool. The weather was perfect, not too hot, not too cold. The sun was shining through palm trees in the

90

cloudless sky. The conversation was good. It was one of those days when your mouth hurt from smiling and laughing so much. Everyone there looked happy, like there was nowhere else they'd rather be. And of course, the drinks were flowing. Well, they were for me. Honestly, I'm not sure how much they were flowing for everyone else, because I never paid much attention to that. I was too busy running my Race to Nowhere, which left little time for considering anything other than my race. Anything that got in the way of my race was nothing more than an annoyance.

Inevitably, on days like this, there comes a point where I would just say, "Fuck it. I'm not working that hard today, I don't want to. I'm going to drink, and I'm going to have fun. Life is short. We're with great friends celebrating a birthday. Iowa won. This isn't the time for hard work. Life is work. I have a demanding job, four kids, I work hard. This is supposed to be vacation, an escape. Can't I just drink and have fun like a normal person? Don't I deserve that? Yes, I do deserve that. Okay, permission granted to let go, have fun, and not work hard. Off we go."

I can't tell you how many drinks I had that afternoon, only that it almost certainly was more than everyone else. When it was time to go back to the rooms and get ready for dinner, I wasn't falling-down drunk. I even might have been able to pass as relatively sober, if you didn't know me (okay, maybe not). Regardless, I was more drunk than you need to be at 5 pm, before dinner. I certainly was more drunk than everyone else. Most people would use the time in between the pool and meeting up for dinner as a time to sober up. Not me. What did I do? Ordered a drink to take back to the room while I showered and got ready for dinner, of course. Why *wouldn't* you do that? Isn't getting ready for a night out more fun when you have a drink in your hand?

My wife left the hotel room to meet up with our group before I was ready to leave—secretly hoping that I would lie down, pass out, and miss dinner altogether. But no such luck. Instead, I showered, changed, and finished the drink I'd brought to the room. When I left the room, I saw an opening to have another drink before I met up with everyone and had to start (in theory) watching myself again. Anytime I was running my Race to Nowhere, any chance I found to get a drink without people knowing was a bonus. It was like free money.

91

Todd Kinney

Walking down to the hotel bar, I happened to run into my college girlfriend, Lisa, the one with the different name from the woman I'd dated early on in law school. I hadn't seen her in fifteen years. She'd recently moved to the Phoenix area and was out with a friend. We had a nice conversation. Meanwhile, I desperately tried to disguise how drunk I was. I'm certain that I wasn't nearly as successful at this as I thought I was at the time. I invited her to come meet my wife and see the Sullivans, who she knew through me. She politely declined. Lisa had had a front-row seat to much of my drinking in college. Here I was, twenty-two years later, married, a lawyer, a dad to four kids—and in the same drunken state in which I'd spent many of my college nights.

"It's a shame you let that one get away" I imagined Lisa's friend saying to her as I walked way, the two of them laughing.

The night got pretty blurry after that. I made my way to the private room where we were eating. My wife, a veteran of my drinking habits, already knew where this was headed. Hell, she had known even before we left the pool. She barely made eye contact with me when I entered the room. I could tell she was annoyed and didn't want to be bothered with my nonsense. If I did catch her looking at me, she would look away abruptly and ever so subtly shake her head back and forth, like she was trying to hide her annoyance from everyone but me. It was clear to me that she had no interest in engaging in any conversation other than one about me going to bed. She would turn away from me if I approached any other conversation she was having.

At one point, she was talking with Clare's husband, Mike. I found out the next day that they were having a conversation about Mike's dad, who recently had been diagnosed with Alzheimer's. It was, as you can imagine, a serious and somber conversation. But all that was lost on me, and I awkwardly barged my way into the conversation completely unaware, acting as if I was joining a conversation about the football game we'd watched earlier in the day. Mike is way too nice a guy ever to tell me that I was being a complete jackass in that moment. But I was being a complete jackass.

As we were milling around waiting for dinner to start, Beth started trying to get me to go back to the room because of how drunk I was.

"You need to go back to the room and go to bed," she said. She was flabbergasted that someone in my state hadn't just stayed in the room in the first place.

I responded with a blank stare. In my mind, this was a preposterous and completely unwarranted suggestion.

"You can barely keep your eyes open!"

"I'm fine! I'm sitting here talking to you, aren't I? I just need to eat dinner, and I'll be fine."

"Is this fun for you?"

"Is what fun? I know this conversation isn't fun, if that's what you're talking about."

"Being this wasted when nobody else is drunk?"

I looked away, annoyed. I didn't like that I had pissed Beth off, but I also wanted her to get off my back. I didn't have much to say. I wanted the conversation to be over. Going to bed would mean admitting defeat, that I once again had failed in my quest to keep my drinking under control, so that wasn't an option. There was still time to save this night.

"Just let me eat dinner and I'll be fine."

Beth looked away and shook her head again, this time with less subtlety. She knew this drill: that I never was as receptive to these suggestions as I should have been. She was embarrassed and irritated. She didn't want me to be her problem, not tonight. All she wanted was to enjoy a night out with good friends.

Despite the frequency of scenes like this, she always was perplexed at my inability to receive and appreciate commonsense suggestions to go home or go to bed because I was too drunk. She never got angry about this—at least, not to the point where it resulted in a blowup fight in the moment. Annoyed and irritated, yes, but not angry. Looking back, I'm surprised she never did. I would have! More often than not, she was in survival mode, where she just wanted to manage the situation without it blowing up into something worse.

Then she leaned over and whispered those words into my ear. "Your parents are staring at you."

I could see my parents out of the corner of my left eye. They were directly across the square table from where Beth and I were sitting. I was turned slightly, facing Beth. I could feel them looking my way, but I didn't look over. I couldn't.

* * *

When I woke up the next morning, those were the first words I heard in my head. "Your parents are staring at you." This time, there was no booze to drown the words out, just a headache. There was no band-aid to cover them up, even temporarily. No numbing agent to dull the effect. They were just sitting in my head, looping over and over. Just when I would think that they were done tormenting me, they would come back. Again and again.

My parents are wonderful people. The last thing they ever would do to someone—especially one of their kids—is shame them. They're just not wired that way. They have more grace and compassion than almost anyone I know. So I knew that they hadn't been looking at me the night before with shame or embarrassment. I never once thought that. Knowing my parents well—and being a parent myself—I had a pretty good idea of what they were feeling as they stared at me across that table while my wife pleaded for me to go to bed. They were sad. They probably were disappointed. Maybe they were worrying about me. Maybe they felt sorry for Beth. But more than anything, I think that, watching me, they were sad.

At that time, I was a forty-four-year-old married man with four kids of my own. I had been out of the house for twenty-six years. My parents long ago had relinquished their parental obligations for me and set me free into the world, as all parents must do at some point. And yet, even then, even as far removed from their care as I was, the thought of my parents looking across the table at their drunk adult son whose wife was pleading with him to go back to the room absolutely wrecked me.

All the shame, all the regret, all the embarrassment, all the "Jesus Christ—again?!" talks with myself . . . I thought I had felt it all. The intensity of the feelings may have varied, but I thought I'd experienced all there was to experience when it came to the cesspool of negativity and self-loathing that accompanied my drinking.

I was wrong. This was new, it was different. It was worse, so much worse. It felt more consequential. The idea of me being responsible for my

94

parents feeling sad about their adult son just gutted me. It was a new level of hell. It made me want to crawl out of my skin. It made me feel two feet tall. It disgusted me. I hated the version of myself who had made my parents feel like that. It left me with a pit in my stomach, and I knew it wasn't going anywhere, and that terrified me. It felt like there was a storm brewing inside my body, and yet the feelings were so gross that I couldn't even bring myself to talk about them. The combination of wanting more than anything in the world to bury those feelings and simultaneously knowing that doing so was impossible was almost too much to bear.

Turns out, that was only gut punch #1 for the day. Gut punch #2 was on the way. Later that morning, the group was gathered around the courtyard, saying our goodbyes. When I turned to my godmother to hug her goodbye, she put both hands on my shoulders, looked me in the face, and said, "Now, what are we going to do about your little problem?"

It was one of those comments that is said—kind of, sort of—as a joke. The people around us who heard it laughed. I smiled uneasily, unsure of what else to do. There was enough truth to it that everyone's laughing felt a little uneasy. Erin, the oldest Sullivan daughter, probably sensing my unease, and tried to defuse the situation. She said, "Oh, leave Todd alone. He was just having fun." And we all chuckled a little more and finished our good-byes. I pretended to shrug it off—which I might have been able to do if not for the torment of having made my parents sad. But in combination? It just piled more bile on an already-overflowing pile of shame. It was like the universe had decided to stop tiptoeing around my drinking. I couldn't get out of there fast enough.

"How many more times are you going to do this? What is it going to take? *What the fuck is it going to take?!*"

The Chinese food restaurant parking lot; walking around downtown Omaha, lost, at 2 am, with a dead phone; Beth telling me she wasn't as attracted to me because of my drinking; not trusting myself; Austin asking whether we needed to take an Uber; the countless morning-after fights, the never-ending wondering and worrying whether I'd said or done something embarrassing the night before; the constant loop of "never again," and then having it happen again; the grogginess, the fog, the work. It was all staring me in the face, and it wasn't going anywhere.

Todd Kinney

I was tired of beating myself up. I was tired of this cycle, period. I didn't want to feel like this again, ever. Something had to change. Real change, not my usual bullshit that lasted for a while but not forever. Enough was enough.

CHAPTER THIRTEEN

Arizona Aftermath

In the days following the Arizona trip, during the brief reprieves from beating the shit out of myself, I would shift into "How are we going to fix this?" mode. I committed to another three-month break from alcohol. It was an easy decision—the intense, tormenting, and shameful feelings I felt from making my parents sad and Ann's comment made me feel out of control, and imposing a three-month break gave me some sense of control over that storm. While I knew deep down that this situation called for something more serious than another three-month break, I wasn't sure exactly what that looked like (or I wasn't quite ready to admit what that looked like). So, the trusty, old three-month break was an easy fallback in the moment. I needed to punish myself, to serve some sort of sentence for my inability to control my drinking (YET AGAIN) in Arizona. The weight of "Your parents are staring at you" and Ann's comment demanded it.

The swiftness of my decision calmed my internal storm a bit, but there was still something brewing inside me that I hadn't felt before. I couldn't sell myself on my own bullshit anymore. It was as if my abusive partner had come to me after yet another episode of beating me up and told me that *this* time it would be different. Except I didn't believe it this time. I couldn't believe it this time. I just didn't have it in me. I had reached my bullshit limit. It wouldn't be different this time. It would be the same old shit that had been going on since the day I picked up my first drink. Because the same old shit always came back. For the first time in my life, I started getting real with myself about my drinking. This time, I told my abusive partner to fuck off.

While the Arizona weekend brought all this to a head abruptly, this reckoning actually had been years in the making. The weekend was *six years* after my first visit to Deanna, at which she'd suggested that I take that first three-month sabbatical. Honestly examining my drinking meant admitting certain things to myself. Not all the things all at once, but little things along the way. I drink differently from others. I need to employ moderation hacks. I don't want to be hung over. I like waking up after a night of not drinking. Things that I'd always known on some level but never said out loud and never examined. Once I admitted them to myself, they became harder to run from, harder to ignore. Eventually, that little voice inside my head became a scream. What started as a slow drip became a full-on tidal wave. Every time I had that one extra drink I wasn't planning on, every time my wife got annoyed with my drinking, every morning that was tinged with feelings of regret and failure, every comment from my kids, every hangover—all of it had been building up. As it was happening, I wasn't really conscious of the progression. But in the days and weeks after the Arizona trip, my tidal wave was making landfall.

The first thing I did after coming home from Arizona was make an appointment with Deanna. I knew I needed to talk to her.

"So, I think I'm going to quit drinking," I texted her.

A couple of weeks later, I went to see her. I still wasn't ready to commit to *forever*, out loud (notice I'd said "I *think*…"), which I'm guessing she sensed, because she suggested that I turn my three-month commitment into a six-month commitment. I agreed to that without hesitation. That seemed easy enough. I had done the three-month thing twice, and that hadn't fully worked, so why not try something different? It felt like a safe middle ground. It gave me that "something different" from what I'd done before that I knew I needed—and for the moment it avoided me having to commit to forever. I also liked it because it bought me more time to explain to everyone what I was doing. It was easier to say "I'm taking a break for six months" than "I'm giving up alcohol forever."

I Didn't Believe It Either

Anytime someone gives up alcohol, there are turning points early on that easily could derail the whole thing. Sometimes they're apparent in the moment, other times they're not. I had one of those moments shortly after returning from Arizona. It was a couple weeks after I'd decided to give up alcohol for at least three months but hadn't committed to forever yet. We were over at some friends' house with other couples and our kids. Everyone ordered takeout. My friend Richard and I went to pick up the food.

Richard was the kind of friend who, if you called him up at 9 am on a Tuesday and told him you needed to go get a drink, he would meet you at the bar. He always made sure you had a full glass. He always ordered the extra bottle of wine. He was always up for one more. He also was one of those guys I always used to feel better about my own drinking.

When we got to the restaurant, the food wasn't ready yet, so the hostess directed us to the bar.

"Looks like we have time for a drink," Richard said. "What do you want?"

The presober me would have been right there with him, of course. But I told him, "Nothing, I'm good." I kept my tone neutral—despite my annoyance. Richard knew damn well I wasn't drinking.

"Oh, come on, man, one beer won't kill you!"

Giving me shit about not drinking was as predictable as him ordering a drink in the first place, so I wasn't surprised by the juvenile peer pressure. But I was surprised when he told the bartender, "We'll have two IPAs," and then set one down right in front of me! There I was, sitting at the bar, with the familiar din of happy hour, a die-hard drinking buddy next to me, and a tall, cold, frothy pint of my favorite beer staring me right in the face, the hoppy aroma begging me to take just one sip.

Instinctively I grabbed the perspiring glass, as I had hundreds of times before—but then I slowly slid it across the wooden bar until it clinked against Richard's glass. "You're an asshole," I said, leaving my untasted beer in front of him. "I told you I'm good."

Some people are weird about their friends not drinking. Some don't know what to say, like when someone dies. Some root for you to fail. That used to really bother me. It made me feel self-conscious, anxious, and awkward. In the beginning, even when nobody said anything about me not drinking, I still felt insecure and vulnerable. When people flipped me shit about it, it preyed on that vulnerability. But eventually I realized that when people do things like buy you a beer and set it in front of you after you've told them you're not drinking, that says nothing about you and everything about them. Me not drinking shone a light on whatever alcohol issues he has—and that's uncomfortable for him. There was a time when I would have been the insensitive jerk giving somebody shit about not drinking. Granted, I wouldn't have been a big enough dick to buy them a drink and set it in front of them. But I would have been annoyed at how their decision to try to make a positive change regarding their drinking made me feel.

***

In those first weeks and months after Arizona, I had some more positive, impactful moments that really helped propel me. I thought of them as signs from the universe that helped light the path for me and offset the awkwardness and uncomfortableness. The first one happened the very first weekend after we got back. It happened in the middle of an otherwise miserable night. On the Friday night following the Arizona weekend, we ended up having an impromptu gathering at our house with some friends and their kids. I was grouchy about not drinking. I didn't necessarily want a drink, but I sure as hell didn't feel like being around a bunch of people drinking and getting drunk. All I wanted was a quiet house so I could go to bed early and get to Saturday morning, which I knew I would enjoy. The last thing I wanted was a house full of people drinking and having fun. Alas, that's exactly what I got.

I hadn't prepared very well for this first sober weekend. I should have known better. I didn't say anything to my wife about what I was feeling or express that I didn't want to do anything that night other than go to bed early. That didn't stop me from getting super annoyed with her for facilitating the impromptu drink-a-thon at our house that night. I was in no mood to socialize or even to fake it. I just didn't have it in me. In hindsight, I should've just gone to bed or left the house and done my own thing, but at that point I was too awkward with my not-drinking to do that. I felt like

---

I needed to show that I could have a good time even though I wasn't drinking. In reality, I wasn't going to have a good time that night. It wasn't because I was physically craving alcohol. I was less than a week out from the Arizona weekend. I was very resolute in my commitment not to drink for at least three months. The act of drinking just wasn't on the table. It wasn't going to happen. But that didn't mean I wanted to hang out with a bunch of people who were drinking and having the time of their lives.

There was a moment later that night, though, that I'm still thankful for to this day. My daughter and her friend came downstairs and announced that they had made up a dance routine that they wanted to show to all of us. Normally, this would have slightly annoyed me. Sure, I would have put a smile on my face and made my daughter and her friend think I was truly excited about seeing their dance routine. Inside, I would have been in a rush to get back to the adult interaction and the main focus of the night—drinking.

This night, however, the dance routine provided a very welcome distraction from trying to fake that I was enjoying myself and from counting the minutes until I could bail on the party to go to bed. In fact, a dance routine sounded downright enjoyable compared with the alternative of watching my adult friends get louder and sloppier. When it was time for the show, Dale (whose daughter was the other performer) and I comprised the entire audience. The girls hit the music and performed their newly produced routine. It was pretty similar to the twenty-five other dance routines we'd seen them do. At one point during the routine, I looked over at Dale, who was sitting to my right on the other couch. His head was back, eyes closed. He was too far away to nudge awake, and I was afraid that if I said something to him the girls would notice that he was asleep. My first thought was, "I hope the girls don't see that Dale is sleeping." My second thought was, "Maybe this sober thing isn't half bad."

It seemed like a small moment at the time. But, looking back, it was a big deal—mostly because it happened that very first weekend, when my head was just a mess. Physically, I was fine with not drinking. Mentally, I couldn't get a good grip on things. I had a hundred thoughts running through my head. Even as committed as I was to another three-month break, and possibly more, not drinking was *always* on my mind. I felt like

I didn't know how to process any of the thoughts that were running through my head. I thought it was going to be like that forever, which just made things worse. That moment gave me a small glimpse into sober life. Being genuinely immersed in my daughter's dance routine instead of nodding off on the couch or being preoccupied with my drinking stuck with me in a good way.

Had I been drinking, I might not even have noticed that my friend was nodding off. I certainly wouldn't have taken the time to process it and to think about the girls' feelings if they noticed. And I myself would not really have been interested in watching them dance. Let's be honest—our kids ask us to watch stuff all the time, and sometimes it's just not that interesting. Sometimes we fake it. But that moment showed me something. It provided something for me. Less than a week into my new three-month (maybe forever) sabbatical, and I saw *it*. Or a slice of *it*: the difference that sobriety could make in my life as a dad. When you stack up being sober for your daughter's dance routine against her watching you nod off, how can you argue against sobriety?

Early in sobriety, we need such moments to keep us going. We need things that keep us coming back. We need thoughts and feelings that we can't shake, that make an impression on us. Seeds that are planted that we can lean on down the road. I got one that night. Not bad, considering how miserable the rest of the night was.

***

About a month later, I had another experience that provided me with some all-important reinforcement that I was doing something good for myself and my family. My wife and I take each of our kids on a trip for their thirteenth birthday. We let them pick the location and plan as much of the trip as they want to. I absolutely love these trips. We get some one-on-one time with our kid—the quality time that is so hard to come by. I look forward to these trips for months.

Landon decided on Los Angeles for his trip. He wanted to go to a Lakers game and an LA Rams game. I actually was relieved that I wouldn't be drinking for this trip. It was always very important to me that my drinking didn't mar occasions like this, like my wife's fortieth birthday party. Usually, I was successful, but it was always *so much work*. So much planning and subsequent effort to stick to that plan. It's funny: a big reason why I wanted to keep my drinking in check was so I could be present for the occasion and enjoy it—to keep the focus on the event and the people I was with. But even when I succeeded at keeping my drinking in check, the work and energy it took to do so ultimately kept me from being fully present anyway. To take drinking off the table meant relief from all that time and energy.

On the Saturday of our trip, we had one of those Top 10 parent-child days that I will remember for a long time. I started the day with an early workout, which I had no problem getting up for because I hadn't drunk the night before. Landon actually did some homework. Then we went for an early lunch at In-N-Out, which was on Landon's list. After that, we headed to an Iowa bar in Santa Monica to watch the Iowa–Minnesota game. Minnesota was 9-0 and ranked seventh in the country. I had promised myself that I wouldn't let an Iowa loss negatively affect the rest of the day. Thankfully, the Hawks won, so I didn't have to worry about that. After the game, we did some shopping and exploring and walked around the Santa Monica pier and the beach. The weather was perfect, and we watched a beautiful sunset from the pier. We found a great little place for dinner near the beach. Landon seemed genuinely to enjoy himself (which is saying something when you're talking about a thirteen-year-old boy). I know Beth and I enjoyed ourselves that day. It's a day I still think about.

At dinner, I was telling Beth how glad I was that I wasn't drinking on this trip.

"Why?" she asked.

I proceeded to tell her how the day would have unfolded had I been drinking. I would've ordered my first drink at the Iowa bar. Wanting to keep things in check for our family trip, I wouldn't have had too many there, but I know that I would've had one or two more than I planned on because Iowa won, and of course that would've called for a celebration. After leaving the bar, I would've spent considerable time and energy calculating when and how I was going to get my next drink. Instead of enjoying shopping and exploring with Landon and being present for that, I would have been plotting places we could stop where I could get a drink.

Instead of getting ice cream with him, I would have suggested ducking into this bar or that bar to take a break from shopping so we could watch some football (and, of course, grab a drink). Or I would've ordered a beer or two while we walked around the pier. Whatever the case, I would have found a way to have a couple drinks while we shopped and explored. I wouldn't have cared that much about seeing the sunset, unless I could do it with a drink in my hand. And when I wasn't actually engaged in the act of drinking, I would've been thinking about drinking, instead of simply enjoying some quality time with my son and wife.

My drinking would've continued at dinner. And then I would've gotten a drink when we got back to the hotel before turning in for the night. In the end, I may not have gotten wasted, but I certainly would have had enough to drink that Landon would have noticed. Same with Beth. And it would've been enough that I'd wake up the next day regretting how much I'd drunk and how much I'd let it rule the previous day. It would've tarnished the entire day. It would've dulled it. It would've turned what is still one of my favorite days with one of my kids into yet another day marred by my drinking. Instead of looking back and smiling about that day, I would look back with some measure of regret and shame.

All this seemed to surprise my wife, which in turn shocked me. She didn't realize that's how my brain worked with alcohol. I'd just assumed that she knew what was going on in my head. It was so all-consuming for me. It was all I knew when it came to drinking. But I never really had described any of this to her. How would she know?

As I reflected on that day and on the trip as a whole, I couldn't get over how happy I was that I wasn't drinking. It was just as much about relief as it was about happiness. I was struck by how good I felt about the trip and myself. Like the moment when my friend nodded off during our girls' dance routine, I caught another glimpse—a longer, more-substantial one this time—of what sobriety had to offer. Another seed was planted. I started to ask myself, "Why would you do anything that would make you feel differently (worse) than this awesome feeling you have right now?" It was the same question my dad had asked himself on Easter morning in 2021.

***

I got another glimpse of "it" about a month after the LA trip. It was December 2019. I had a trip planned to New York City with three buddies. One I had known since middle school, one was my best friend from college, and the other was a life-long friend of my college friend, who I had gotten to know very well over the years. They're all great guys. We were going to New York for a Bud Crawford fight. Bud is a world-champion boxer from Omaha who I represented for a time.

Part of me was glad that I wasn't drinking on this trip. It was partly a work trip, and while I never drank on the clock it was always an internal battle for me on these trips. I was out of town (usually in NYC or Vegas) and it seemed like everyone else was drinking, so I always would be somewhat resentful that I couldn't drink when everyone else seemed to be. It was a lot of work, and it seemed like I spent a lot of my time counting the minutes until whatever the magic hour was when it became okay for me to start drinking. So, like the LA trip with Landon and Beth, taking it out of play was kind of a relief.

But I also was very nervous about the trip. I was so new in my sobriety that it still was very raw. I wasn't worried about drinking—I was feeling very much committed, even though I hadn't decided how long my break would be. But I was worried that I wouldn't have a good time. I was worried that my buddies wouldn't have a good time because the sober guy would hold them back. Like my nondrinking would follow us around Manhattan like a dark rain cloud and transform everything we did from the best time ever to meh. I thought my buddies would give this trip a try because they're nice guys, only to start planning secret future trips without me so they actually could enjoy themselves. I thought the trip would be divided into halves: one half with me and my non-drinking that they just "got through," and the other half without me where all the laughs, funny stories, and life-long memories would be made.

Like so many things I imagined when I thought about what a life of sobriety would look like, my concerns could not have been more off base. I felt more connected to my buddies than I had in a long time—certainly more connected than on guys' trips where the drinks were flowing. The conversations were better (for one, I remembered all of them), and the time we spent together was more fulfilling. It felt more genuine. I didn't have any regrets when I woke up in the morning. I didn't have to ask them how we ended the night or how we got back to the hotel. I didn't spend half the day nursing a hangover or getting back to level. I didn't have to worry about whether I'd done or said something embarrassing. On some previous trips like this I would return home and feel like I'd spent about five good minutes with my friends, because the whole weekend was a blur of drinking and partying. Not this time—and I loved it. I also didn't need two days just to recover once I got home.

On the Friday morning of the trip, I got up early and walked to Central Park for a run. Central Park is one of my favorite spots on earth. As I finished my run, a feeling of exhilaration and gratitude washed over me like I'd never experienced before. It came out of nowhere. It startled me and amazed me at the same time. Runners talk about a "runner's high"—it sort of felt like that, but on steroids. My senses were heightened—the air felt crisper, the sky looked brighter. I was overcome with joy, and I wasn't sure why. I felt like I could float back to the hotel. I took it as a message from the universe telling me to keep going. It was telling me I was on the path I was meant to be on. I remember thinking, "I have to bottle this feeling. I want to remember it forever." I knew I would never want to drink again if I could remember that feeling. I took a picture of the park in that moment to document what I was feeling. It was the only way I knew to at least try to capture the moment so I could come back to it later, which I knew I would want to do. Another seed was planted.

On Sunday morning, I walked over to Bryant Park. It was perfect December weather—just brisk enough to feel like the holidays, but warm enough that it was still enjoyable to be outside. I strolled by the merchant booths and took in the Christmas decorations. I looked for a Christmas present for my mom, who is nearly impossible to buy for because she has everything. I watched people ice skate. I smiled as I saw kids having fun. I just soaked it all in. I bought a coffee and took a seat right by the ice-skating rink that was shadowed by the tall buildings on each side. I took out my phone to text my therapist.

"Good morning, Deanna. I'm finishing a long weekend
in NYC with three buddies. I need to write more about this

on my own, but just wanted to let you know how happy I am with the non-drinking path I'm on. Before the trip, I wondered how I'd feel about this weekend. I had a great time. It was the right group of friends who are supportive, etc. I had a moment on Friday morning after a run in Central Park where I just felt so good about what I'm doing. I need to bottle that feeling!"

Deanna: "This is outstanding! Journal about your gains, clarity, and peace you are experiencing. Sounds like you are liking yourself more sober. Stay the course!"

Her words "Sounds like you are liking yourself more sober" stopped me in my tracks. I read them again, and then a third time. Holy shit, I thought. She's right! I *am* liking myself more! *That* is what I'm feeling.

I always had considered myself to be pretty healthy on the self-esteem scale. I never thought I had any issues liking myself. But I had no idea what effect my drinking had on things like that. Of course, I was well acquainted with the feelings of shame, embarrassment, and regret. I knew what those were, and I knew that my drinking led to those feelings too often. I knew I didn't like it when those feelings appeared. But I never really connected all that to making me like myself less. I thought they were just stand-alone emotions that came and went. But they didn't come and go. They stayed, deep inside me. And eventually, they started to set up shop. Quietly at first, so I didn't even know they were there. But they were. And they all joined hands and connected to each other. Over time, they grew stronger together. As they grew stronger, they slowly, quietly, chipped away at that healthy self-esteem I'd always had.

Here's the thing: I didn't realize any of this until I stopped drinking. At this point—the trip to New York—I hadn't committed fully to quitting for good. But I was in a mode where I was examining everything. I wanted to collect all the data that came with (possibly) quitting so I eventually could throw it all on the scale and see which way it tipped. Deep down, I knew which way it was going to tip. I just had to get to the point where I wasn't freaked out by the result. Sometimes you have to step away from something—for some amount of time, if not forever—to see clearly. This is why breaks from alcohol, no matter how long, can be so beneficial, if you're willing to do some self-examination. It allows you to see things that you simply can't see when you're in the thick of it.

I'm so thankful that trip happened when it did, early on in my process. I'm thankful for the friends I went with. I'm thankful for the text from my therapist. I'm thankful for that euphoric feeling I got running in Central Park that was so powerful that I knew it was signaling something to me that I couldn't ignore. More than anything, I'm thankful that I did that trip sober, because the realization that I was liking myself more as a nondrinker was huge for me. How do you go back to something after you've discovered that you like yourself more without it?

About a year and a half after that trip, I was texting with one of the friends I'd gone with. I mentioned how much that trip had meant to me on my sober journey, and how he and the other two friends were big reasons for that.

"I loved that trip so much," he texted back.

CHAPTER FOURTEEN

Calling It Quits

The question "Am I an alcoholic?" kept me stuck for a long time. It was the same as asking, "Do I have a drinking problem?" I didn't want to be labeled an *alcoholic* (at least not how I defined it in my mind), so I spent a lot of time convincing myself that I wasn't. Until one day it just hit me: none of those labels mattered. It didn't matter if I met the clinical definition of *alcoholic*. It didn't matter if I was *not* an alcoholic. What does that term even mean, anyway? What mattered more than anything was that alcohol had gotten to the point where the positive/negative ratio was too imbalanced. It was two hours of fun versus twenty-two hours (or more) of feeling like crap physically, and all the emotional baggage that came along with it. Alcohol was having a negative impact on my life, to the point where I wanted to change what I was doing. That was the beginning, middle, and end of the analysis. Label it whatever you want—"alcoholic," "issues with alcohol," "bad relationship with alcohol," "gray-area drinker," "alcohol-use disorder." Whatever. None of that mattered. What mattered was that I wanted to make a change.

The question then became, "What does that change look like?" Up to that point, the answer always had been some form of moderation, trying the latest, greatest idea I'd come up with to control my drinking. But the moderation experiment had run its course. The results were in—they actually had been in for some time.

Moderation didn't work for me for the same reasons that it doesn't work for anyone who has issues with alcohol. When you have an unhealthy relationship with alcohol, moderating your drinking is a shit ton of work. It takes an enormous amount of time and energy. It occupies an inordinate amount of headspace. I found it exhausting—and that's when it was going well. Moderation, when it worked, kept the bad at bay—the shame, the guilt, the remorse. Those feelings were so heavy that lifting them should have been life changing. But it wasn't, because the burden was replaced by the weight of moderating. It was still a prison, just a different set of walls.

The turning point for me was finally accepting that moderating didn't work. For years I'd held on to the illusion that "if I could only do X, I could drink like a normal person. If I just try harder, I can drink like a normal person." The reality was, there was no "X." There was no amount of trying that could make it work. There never had been. I might as well have been trying (over and over and over again) to find the secret to make me 6'3" instead of 5'10". I was fighting an unwinnable battle. Until one day I stopped fighting. I gave up.

I still remember the day I surrendered. I was alone in my car. It was about four months into my post-Arizona sabbatical. Drinking thoughts were bouncing around inside my head, as they did during most of my waking moments in this period. All of a sudden, it crystalized for me. I said something to myself I'd never admitted before.

"You can't control your drinking. Not to the extent that you want to or the extent that will make you happy. No matter what you try, you can't do it. IT'S. NOT. POSSIBLE."

I didn't fight it this time. I didn't rationalize it. I didn't try to caveat my way out of this indisputable conclusion that had been staring me in the face for some time. Instead, I accepted it and surrendered to it. It felt really damn good—much better than I expected. It was so liberating. As I sat in my car, I instantly felt lighter, like a boulder had been removed from my chest. I felt like crying.

Once I made this acceptance, the path forward opened up for me magically. The confusion, the difficulty, the haze, the internal debate, the resistance—it all melted away. It was like that missing piece of the puzzle that suddenly makes the rest of the puzzle easy to put together. If I couldn't control my drinking, there was only one option if I truly wanted to change—which, by that point, I desperately did. And that was to quit. It just became so simple for me. I smiled as I drove by myself in my car that day. Quitting for good was still scary, but the surrender felt so good and so right that the fear didn't matter as much. Sometimes, surrender is the only way you truly can move forward.

As painful as those teenage lessons were that my parents were so intent on teaching me, they paid off later in life. They helped form the make-up that eventually led me to quit drinking. I reached a point where, deep down, I knew "the right thing" was to give up drinking. The battle in my mind between "the right thing" and the easy thing had been intense and unrelenting. It went on for years. And for years, the easy thing won out. I was always relieved when I talked myself out of quitting altogether. It was a reprieve from a prison sentence. It was all too much and too damn hard to take on the right thing. Too scary, too much work, too much uncertainty. As hard as moderating was, it still was the easier way out. It was nothing compared to how hard the idea of quitting seemed.

But eventually, the right thing won out. I got sick of choosing the easy thing, because eventually it stopped serving me. I got sick of the little voice in my head criticizing me for taking that easy way out. I decided to take on all the shit that comes with doing the right thing. I just had to get to the point where the scales tipped toward the right thing. But to do that, I had to have the compass pointing me in the right direction in the first place. I had that compass, thanks in large part to my parents and the lessons they let (made!) me learn, from the mailbox baseball, disturbing the peace, and test stealing. My teacher was right: I am incredibly grateful for it all.

Even after I admitted my realization to myself, I still wasn't ready to say it out loud. I knew I needed to tell Beth, because once I did that there truly was no going back. I would be a fraud. She would know it. But more than that, I would know it. I needed to explain to her the reasons why I needed to quit for good. I needed to say those things out loud. Once I explained to her that I had come to the conclusion that it was the best decision for me, our marriage, and our family—once I said those words out loud to her—how could I go back? That would be going back on me, her, and our family. It would be a middle finger to all of that, to the very people and things I cared about most. It would be the official, unmistakable confirmation that I cared about alcohol more than myself and my family. What kind of asshole does that? I was pretty certain I wasn't going to be that asshole, but first, I had to say those things out loud to her.

All this bounced around in my head for at least a week before I said the words out loud. You know when you're little (or even when you're an adult) and you know you need to get something off your chest? Maybe you told a lie and you need to come clean, or you just need to clear your conscience about something? That feeling in your gut that you need to do something, but you just can't muster up the courage to say whatever it is you need to say? You start the process of doing so about ten times, but you always find an excuse not to follow through? That's what that week felt like.

Finally, it was time. Beth was sitting at the island in our kitchen. I was in our bedroom. It was a short walk from our bedroom to the kitchen, but on this day it took me a long time to make it. I got to the doorway of the kitchen three times and turned around before I actually walked all the way in. One time I walked back to the bedroom. The other times I walked halfway and just paced the hallway. What was I afraid of? Stop being such a pussy, I told myself.

I slowly walked into the kitchen and stood at the corner of the island. Beth was to my right, sitting down, reading a magazine. She didn't look up. I wished she would look up to give me some sort of prompt.

"So." [A couple seconds of silence]. This reminded me of the sex conversation, when I wished she knew what I was about to say and would just say it for me.

"I think I need to give up alcohol for good."

"Really?" she replied, without much emotion.

Did she not hear what I just said?!

"Well, I realized I'll never be able to control my drinking to the extent I want to. I can keep it in check for periods of time, but never for the long haul. I just can't, no matter how badly I want to or how hard I try."

No response from Beth. What did this mean? Why wasn't she saying anything? I didn't dwell on that because I was focused on just getting the words out. I needed to get all of it out.

"Plus, there are so many things I like about not drinking. I think giving it up for good is just something I need to do."

"Okay," she finally said.

It seemed like one of those "okays" you give when someone who never goes to the gym regularly tells you they're going to start going to the gym every day. Maybe she didn't believe me. Maybe she just didn't grasp the magnitude of what I was declaring. Or maybe it was a combination of both. Whatever the case, at the time I wasn't too concerned with her (non) reaction. I couldn't believe how much better I felt after saying all that out loud. It was just like what I'd felt while driving a week earlier, only more intense. I felt lighter, like I could breathe again. I felt relief. I experienced the inner peace and affirmation that comes with knowing you've done the right thing, even if it felt weird and terrifying. I'd needed that. I was still scared shitless about giving up alcohol forever, but in that moment I felt at peace with the decision. Now I just needed to figure out how I was going to do life as a nondrinker.

CHAPTER FIFTEEN

Early Sobriety: The Storm

L ife didn't magically get better after I committed to giving up alcohol forever. In a lot of ways, that was when the real work began. Early sobriety can be awkward, lonely, and depressing. Sometimes it can be all those things at once. For someone with obsessive tendencies like me, it also can be all-consuming. I thought about it *all the time*. One of our first social events in early sobriety was a night out with friends at a bar. My mind raced every time I contemplated the night out. Before we even left the house, I spent hours thinking about how things would unfold. Most people who would be there knew I was not drinking (although none of them knew I'd decided to make it forever). What if someone asks me what I want to drink? What will I say if someone asks why I'm not drinking? Should I tell them I'm giving it up for good? Will it be awkward? What if someone gives me shit about it? What will they think about me? Will people still talk to me? What *am* I going to drink if I'm not drinking alcohol? Should I have lime with water to make it look like a drink? A nonalcoholic beer? What if someone hears me order an NA beer at the bar?! These thoughts raced through my mind on a loop.

When we walked into the bar, I felt like I had a huge, flashing, neon sign following me around that said "This guy isn't drinking. You should ask him about it!" I thought it was tattooed on my forehead, that everyone knew it, and that everyone was wondering what the hell was wrong with me. I was just waiting for someone to say something, and I was convinced I would make a mess of my response. I was pretty sure that the only reason anyone came to that bar that night was to discuss the fact that I wasn't drinking. The awkwardness and anxiety took me back to how it felt when I attended my first junior high dance.

We found our friends and sat down at the table. The unease and anxiety of the ordering process hit me the moment we sat down. The first thing I did was take note of what everyone else was drinking. Yep, looked like everyone else had a drink, and that I would be the ONLY person not drinking alcohol. It was a big table—probably ten or twelve people at it. The waiter was at the opposite end of the table when he started taking orders. Holy shit, was he going to stay there for everyone's order? If so, I might as well announce my nonalcoholic order over the loudspeaker for the entire bar to hear. Please tell me he's going to walk around the table as he takes everyone's order! Luckily, he came fairly close. I wanted an NA beer, but the possibility of someone overhearing me ask for that was too much for me. So I ordered a water. I resisted the urge to whisper my order directly into his ear. But, no comments from anyone else at the table. Whew.

The rest of the night was mostly fine. None of the conversations that I'd played out in my head over and over again actually happened. A couple of people asked me about not drinking, but I didn't have any prolonged conversations about it. I didn't have intense physical cravings to drink that night (I was fortunate that I didn't have a lot of physical cravings in general). But the psychological desire to drink was strong. To feel like I fit in. To quiet my racing mind. To do something to ensure that all the questions I was fearing didn't come my way. To stop feeling different from everyone else. I felt insecure and, on some level, I wanted a drink to make that feeling go away. But I didn't drink.

The next morning, I felt like a million bucks, both physically and mentally. In early sobriety, it was the mornings that began to drive me. I *loved* mornings after not drinking the night before. Physically, of course, waking up after not drinking feels a hundred times better than waking up after a night of imbibing. But the real payoff for me was the mental side of things. Waking up without any shame or regret from the night before is priceless. Waking up without the nagging anxiety of having done or said something embarrassing feels fantastic. Waking up and not beating myself up for failing to keep it in check the night before is liberating. The pride I felt in myself was something I couldn't get enough of. I loved all of it so much that I couldn't wait for my next sober morning. I didn't know it was possible to wake up feeling these things. I started wanting those more than I wanted to drink the night before. Knowing how I would feel the next morning got me through many a night early on in sobriety.

Early sobriety is a fascinating and dumbfounding combination of emotions. I call it "the Storm." My presobriety idea of what the Storm would look like centered exclusively around the physical desire to drink and the difficulty of staving off cravings. I assumed that would be the hardest part. But for me, the physical cravings ended up being one of the easier parts. I never did have that moment where I felt like I was a split second away from cracking a bottle open. I had some moments, sure, but never a close call where I had to be talked off the ledge.

But that wasn't what made the Storm so confounding. The hardest parts were all things I never saw coming. On the one hand, I had the intoxicating pride and clearheadedness of my sober mornings that I couldn't get enough of. I had a feeling of accomplishment that fueled me. I had the little voice in my head telling me I was on the right path. And I had a newfound sense of gratitude that was far and away greater than any buzz alcohol ever had given me. At the same time, I was plagued with bouts of loneliness, awkwardness, self-doubt, and insecurity—all things I wasn't really used to. I didn't understand how something that made me feel so good also could make me feel so unsure and tentative.

It prompted this recurring question that kept popping up in my head: Where was this life of sobriety taking me? I knew, on the whole, that it was good for me. I knew, in my heart of hearts, that it was what I needed to do. But it also felt like I was being left behind—relegated to a life that would be nice, but a little duller. A little boring and awkward. If sobriety was so good for me—and there were times when it unmistakably felt like what I was meant to do—then what was the deal with all these feelings of unease, uncomfortableness, and awkwardness? I waffled between "this feels so good!" and being sad because I felt alone and uncertain. Had I known then how much I would end up enjoying a sober life, none of this would have mattered.

But of course, that's not how it works. Early sobriety can be lonely as hell. At times, it felt like I was the only person on earth who didn't drink or was trying to give up drinking. Even the people closest to me didn't "get" what I was going through, and that made the loneliness worse. Everywhere I went, people looked like they were having the time of their lives drinking. When I quit, I didn't know anyone in our social circle who didn't drink. Hell, I only knew of my dad and one other person I'd gone to law school with who didn't drink. That was it, out of the entire universe of people I knew. I felt like I was on an island.

It can be depressing because it feels like the awkwardness and loneliness are going to be there forever. It doesn't last forever, but it feels like that in the moment. It's also depressing, because you feel like you're missing out on all the fun. I was convinced that my life would be less fun and that people would stop wanting to hang out with me. I looked at people drinking, and I romanticized it. I would get irritable at the thought of going out and not being able to drink. "Why me?!" I would ask myself. "This is bullshit! Why does he get to drink and I don't? He has way more of a problem than I do! This isn't fair!" I had a lot of pity parties for myself. I would get mad at my wife over all this, like it was her fault that we were going out and I couldn't drink. We had a lot of stupid little fights over things that actually had nothing to do with whatever we supposedly fought over. It was just me being pissed that I wasn't drinking anymore when the rest of the world was.

I was so hung up on the idea of forever. FOREVER?! Do you know how long that is?! Why would I want to commit to anything forever? Especially something that, at times, felt like a punishment? Giving it up for three or six months at a time is one thing. You know you're going back. So the focus is on just getting by until that predetermined period is up. There's that light at the end of the tunnel. I can do just about anything for a set amount of time if I know there's a finish line and a goal to be accomplished. In fact, I love the feeling of setting a goal and accomplishing it. But if you take that finish line out of the picture, things start to get real. There's no light at the end of the tunnel (or at least it feels like that for a while). There's no "getting by" until some magical date. So when the awkwardness of not drinking hit or the feelings of missing out set in, I couldn't tell myself, "Just get through this, it won't last long, you'll be drinking again in two weeks." Now it was, "How am I going to do this for the rest of my life?" In the moment, it seems like every social situation is going to be this way. That's a shitty feeling. Who wants to live like that?

These pity parties, the awkwardness, the dread of social events that wouldn't involve drinking, the illusion that everyone else in the world is having the best time they've ever had because they're drinking—all that sometimes made my decision to stop drinking feel like a punishment. Sometimes I felt like I was serving a sentence for not being able to drink like a normal person. A lifetime sentence of "fear of missing out." It wasn't fair. It pissed me off. It never really made me question my decision (although that's very common), but it irritated me at times.

As Laura McKowen says in her second book, *Push Off from Here*:

> "Things are always an invitation to a deeper way of living, but they never feel that way. They feel like problems. They feel like injustices. They feel like loss and anger and frustration. They feel personal and unfair. They feel like shit." [3]

These were only moments in time. Looking back, it's easier to see them as snapshots, as temporary feelings rather than a new reality. At the time, though, they felt heavy. Really heavy.

There were a couple times after I committed to quitting when the voice showed up in my head trying to convince me that I was overreacting. Some people even give this voice a name. I remember one time in particular. I was driving home and pulled off at the exit that I normally took to get home. It was overcast and gray out. This stretch of road had been cleared for a massive development project. But for now, it was all dirt and gray sky. The brown, wooden utility poles were the only things that dotted the landscape. The lingering Midwest winter had me dreaming about an upcoming trip to California. That's when the voice started.

"Why don't you try just drinking on vacation when the kids aren't around? What's the harm in that? If things get out of control, your kids won't see you. They'll never know. Vacations are made for drinking! Why would you want to go on vacation and *not* drink?"

"Maybe you could drink when you go out for dinner. You know, when the kids aren't around. Two drinks maximum. No exceptions. How could you ever get in trouble if you limit it to two drinks?"

"If you limit your drinking to when the kids aren't around and you're not going to see them that night, they'll never see you drunk. That's a big thing that bothers you about your drinking. So you'd be 'fixing' that problem. Who cares what your drinking looks like if your kids don't see it? This new method would fix 95% of your drinking issues. Isn't that enough?"

"You want to fix this bad enough that you will manage it this time."

That inner voice showed up because drinking is addictive and because I was scared to give it up. For any alcoholic, even after he quits, there's a long time when a part of the brain wonders, is it really necessary to totally quit? Laura McKowen calls it the third door: one that sits between drinking in the manner that's causing issues and quitting altogether. It's our fears and insecurities talking to us.

Whenever this voice showed up, the one thing that always slapped me back into reality was my kids. I knew, beyond a shadow of a doubt, that if I stuck with quitting, my kids would be better off. I would be setting a good example, and my relationship with them would improve. In my gut, I knew that to be true. How do you argue with that? How do you choose drinking over an alternative that you know is guaranteed to be a good thing for your kids? When I focused on that, it became easier to shut that inner voice down.

At some point around the six-month mark, I read something about quitting that helped flip a switch for me. Someone described quitting drinking as a legitimate grieving process, just like when you lose a loved one. At first, this seemed so odd to me—almost silly. Losing a loved one is real, actual grief. We're *supposed* to grieve the loss of loved ones. But how can you feel grief over a *thing*, like alcohol? Plus, I was giving it up because I'd failed to control it. This is what I deserved, right? Was I even allowed to grieve?

The more I thought about it, though, the more it made perfect sense. Drinking was a friend who'd been by my side for twenty-five years. It was there for everything—good times, bad times, happy times, sad times. Every momentous occasion in my life, every vacation, every family get-to-gether, every dinner with friends, every work function, every tailgate, every happy hour, every airport, every mundane Friday night, every sporting event, every dinner out, every memory. And everything in between. You name it, alcohol was by my side.

So it makes sense that I was grieving its loss. Even if it had brought bad things into my life, it still was something that had "been there" with me for over two decades. It was ingrained into just about every part of my life. Once I looked at it through the lens of grieving, it made it so much easier to understand why I was having the thoughts I was having. It made the Storm easier to weather. From then on, I was able to let my feelings work through me and eventually move on from them. That small, yet significant, shift in perspective completely cleared the way to process what I was experiencing. Once I did that, I wasn't annoyed or sad that I didn't drink anymore. Now I'm a little sad that I didn't give it up sooner.

CHAPTER SIXTEEN

The Storm: Marriage Edition

In addition to the Storm, another challenge that completely blindsided me was the effect that my quitting had on my marriage. This was a different kind of storm: one made up of a lack of connection, a perceived lack of support, and panic over whether my marriage was compatible with my new life of sobriety.

I am hardwired to connect with people. I thrive on it, it gives me energy. One of the first things I like to do when something is on my mind is to talk to someone about it. When I hear about someone doing something inspirational or going through something traumatic, I want to reach out to that person and let them know that I found their story to be inspiring or find out more about their trauma. I've always been this way.

Beth, on the other hand, is not a connection person. I've known this for a long time. But this difference never had manifested itself so forcefully until I got sober. Looking back, I now realize that this had been more of an issue with us than I ever truly understood. But in my first six to eight months of sobriety, it was staring me right in the face. There was a spotlight on it. I needed to connect with people over sobriety. I looked to my wife to be one of those persons, but she wasn't filling that role. In hindsight, expecting her to be able to do that was unrealistic and unfair. But in the moment, I really needed that connection, and I resented that I wasn't getting it.

One thing I knew from my journey from "my alcohol use is an issue" to "I need to change the way I drink" to "I need to give up drinking forever" was that this spotlight on the connection issue with my wife was not going anywhere. I could choose to ignore it. I could choose to push it back down into my subconscious. But it would be coming back. In some way, shape, or form, it would come back. I was certain of this. That's why it unnerved me so much.

I felt like Beth's attitude was, "This is your issue—you figure it out. You're the one who stopped drinking, who changed this whole deal between us, so you figure out how to rework our social life without it affecting me." But what I wanted was for *us* to figure it out. I wanted to hear her say, "I get it. Let's figure this out together." I didn't hear that or feel it from her.

I didn't know how to figure it out—it was all so weird and different from what we were used to in our previous twenty years together. Hell, I wasn't even sure what I wanted, or what this new sober life should look like. I didn't have any answers, and neither did she. There was no road map. But I thought she didn't care enough even to *try* to find the answers, and she thought my "answer" was a complete overhaul of how we lived and socialized. Both beliefs were unfounded, but neither of us knew that at the time.

My connection crisis was tied up in resentment at what I felt was a lack of support from Beth. I really wanted to hear her say that she was proud of me. But in the first six months, she never said that once. After that, the only time she mentioned it was when I would tell her that I thought it was odd that she'd never said it to me. "Of course I'm proud of you," she would reply. We all know how those kinds of comments feel.

Once she said, "It just doesn't seem like it's that difficult for you."

"Are you fucking kidding me?!" I screamed inside my head. Here I was, doing something that at one point seemed impossible, for the betterment of me, her, our marriage, and our family. It may not have seemed like it from the outside, but giving up drinking felt every bit as all-encompassing as drinking did—probably more so. It consumed me just like drinking had. Was it asking too much for her just to express that she was proud of me for taking on that challenge? I wanted her to say that she understood how hard this was for me at times. I wanted a pat on the back.

And I wanted all this without having to ask for it. But I wasn't getting any of that from her.

I wanted all those things from her because that's how I express support to others. And that's also how I'm used to receiving it. I had a very specific expectation of how my wife should show me support. And if that wasn't met exactly how I imagined it should be, I was incredibly disappointed. But my wife doesn't express support that way. Her way of expressing support is by trying to help you figure out how to get something from point A to point B. She approaches things like this in a very practical way. Want to quit drinking? Then just quit drinking. It's that simple to her. If it's not that simple, then what do you need to do to accomplish it? Okay, then do that. Her idea of support is walking you through that process. It couldn't be any different from my idea of support.

I'll give you a perfect illustration of how we tackle problems and support differently. In 2022, a loved one was going through a traumatic situation and needed to get out of an abusive relationship as soon as possible. She had gotten to the emergency room after her husband broke her arm. My first thought was, "I need to hug this person and tell her that we love her and will be there for her with whatever she needs." Beth's reaction was literally to plan every step of her escape from the relationship, to direct this loved one in what to do. From buying plane tickets to legal considerations to making living arrangements after the escape, Beth figured it all out and laid it out for the loved one. It's a valuable skill to have in situations like that—one that is not "front of mind" for me. It's also only one side of the coin.

Beth doesn't like to rely on people for emotional support. She didn't receive much of it growing up, so she figured out how to do life without it, which meant not asking for it. She decided early on that she wasn't ever going to need someone in her life for her to accomplish what she wanted. She wasn't going to be dependent on anyone. She's very proud of that, and she should be. Beth has accomplished almost everything in her life *despite* a lack of support, whereas I've achieved almost everything because of life-long support from family and friends. To her, emotional support isn't always front of mind, because she's accomplished so much without it. To me, it's everything. When you put two people like that together, it's an interesting mix.

Mind you, all this was going on inside my head. I wasn't sharing any of it with Beth—at least not yet. I was having all sorts of imaginary conversations in my head. I was inventing things that Beth would say (or not say) in response to my grievances, and then I was getting worked up over those imaginary responses. Of course, nothing was getting resolved.

When I did come out and ask for more support, it almost always ended in some sort of argument. My wife would say she was supporting me. I would say she wasn't. Back and forth we'd go. Sometimes when you're giving up alcohol, you just need someone to put their arm around you or give you a hug and say, "I know this is hard. I'm proud of you." I had made a major life decision, in large part to improve our marriage and our family. I was floundering with parts of this new life, even though I was at peace with the decision generally. And I felt like I was doing this alone, without the one person who should have been by my side the entire way.

Beth, meanwhile, was carrying 20 years of resentment over my drinking. All she wanted, from the day we met, was for me to drink like a normal person. Was that so much to ask? Just don't be the drunkest one in the room. Don't be the one passing out at the table while we wait for dinner. Don't be the one who has to go home early. Don't be the one who embarrasses her. Don't be the one about whom everyone asks, "What happened to him?" Don't be the one she has to worry about every time we go out, or every time I go out with friends. She endured so many nights when my drinking ruined the night for her, intruded on her ability to enjoy herself, or simply embarrassed her. Each time it happened, she would grow more desperate for me to figure it out and more exasperated that I couldn't.

It was inconceivable to her that I, an adult man, had not "learned" the skill of drinking like a normal person. To her, it was like someone growing up and not knowing how to read. She just wanted us to be a normal, social couple that could drink together without the cloud of angst that followed her everywhere. She didn't realize, of course—and neither did I for the longest time—that there was no "figuring it out" for me. There was no magic formula. I never would drink like a normal person.

When I finally figured *that* out, it felt like I was pulling the rug out from under her when I decided to quit. She wanted a normal drinking husband, not a nondrinking one. This was a different ball game. Her mind was racing just as much as mine.

What did all this mean?
Why doesn't he want to go anywhere anymore?
What the hell are we going to do for a social life now?
Are we going to stop being invited places?
Will our friends abandon us?
Will the two of us ever be able to have fun again?
Did my husband just become super boring?

Beth's questions weren't any different from the ones I'd been asking myself. When I realized that, all of a sudden her muted reaction to me telling her that I was going to quit made more sense.

My marriage felt unsteady. I felt like I was floating between two worlds, in no man's land. I no longer was connected to my drinking world, where my wife resided, yet I wasn't feeling connected to this new sober world that I was trying to join, where my wife did not reside. I didn't know who I was exactly. I felt like I didn't have a home. Beth was acting as if all I was doing was giving up pizza, while also silently panicking about what this change meant for our marriage.

I was internalizing all this and "worst case scenario-ing" it, as I tend to do. I had decided that Beth just wasn't that supportive of a person, and I had to figure out whether I could live with that. I didn't know that I could. More generally, I didn't know what my new "home" was going to look or feel like, or where Beth fit in there. For the first time that I could remember, I started questioning whether our marriage could continue to work. I didn't know whether the sober version of me was compatible with Beth. That scared the shit out of me.

Not getting the support I needed at home, I found it elsewhere, pretty much by accident. During one session with my therapist around this time, she told me, "You're doing this alone. You need a community." I resisted, even though she was 100% right.

"I'm fine," I said. "I've gone six months without alcohol. I'm not having intense cravings. I know this is the right decision for me. I'm enjoying it—mostly. I've got this."

Deanna, because she's a pro and knows me well, didn't push. Instead, she recommended Laura McKowen's book *We Are the Luckiest: The Surprising Magic of a Sober Life.* [4]If you haven't read it, I can't recommend it enough. I had no idea how desperately I needed it, but I read it at the perfect time and it was a game changer for me. I nodded along to most of it. It was the first time I felt like there was someone out there besides me who struggled with alcohol in the way that I did. I identified so much with how she seemed to have things together on the outside but couldn't shake her internal battle with her drinking. It was the first time I felt like there was someone else out there who understood what I was going through. The book helped me realize that getting sober is about *gaining* so much rather than giving something up. Laura has a special gift for putting the perfect words to the struggle of quitting and the beauty of recovering.

When COVID hit, McKowen started The Luckiest Club (TLC), an online sober-support community that consisted of a Facebook group and daily Zoom meetings. You could sit back and lurk, not even turning your camera on if you didn't want to. Or you could raise your hand virtually and share. I attended meetings for several weeks before I garnered the courage to speak up for the first time. Once I did, I cringed at what I ended up saying. I don't think it made much sense or was very eloquent. But I kept showing up. Every time I attended one of those meetings, I realized I wasn't alone. Each time I logged on, I saw 200 to 250 people doing the same thing I was doing: trying to address their issues with alcohol. Every time someone spoke up, they said something that resonated with me. Every time someone told their story, I heard a part of mine in it. I found it to be a place of so much compassion and support. There was no judgment. Who was going to judge? We were all there because we struggled with alcohol. It felt safe. It felt good. It felt like the home I needed at the time. I made connections with people there who I'm still friends with today.

When you meet someone in recovery, no matter how different your backgrounds may be, you instantly have something in common with them. It's more than the common bond that might result from liking the same football team, living in the same town, or having some other shared interest. It's different—deeper than almost anything else. It's like you both know a secret language. That makes the connection instantaneous, strong, and genuine.

The other thing about the recovery community that I absolutely love is that there's zero bullshit. It's so refreshing. The people are raw, vulnerable, and honest. Nobody is trying to impress anyone else. We're leading with things we feel a lot of shame and embarrassment over. That disarms everyone and fosters an environment of comfort and compassion. We all need more of that in our lives. With TLC, I finally was getting the connection I'd been missing and craving. Shared experiences, plus support and recognition from people who understood. I knew it was going to be an important part of my journey going forward.

While all that felt good, I also had this weird feeling that I was doing something wrong—almost like I was cheating on Beth. I even hid my involvement with TLC from her at first. I had this nagging thought: "Shouldn't I be getting this support from the people closest to me instead of (or at least in addition to) these online strangers?" And if I wasn't getting it from the people close to me, did that mean that my relationship—mainly the one with my wife—was in trouble?

When it comes to alcohol, a lot of people in your life just won't "get it." If they don't have issues with alcohol, it's impossible to understand how we who do think about alcohol. They simply can't grasp how our brains work when it comes to drinking. It's like when I told my wife how that day in southern California with our son would have gone if I'd been drinking. It blew her mind when she heard how I much I would have been thinking about alcohol and my drinking that day. Normal drinkers just don't think about alcohol all the time.

It's okay to go outside your regular circle for support. In fact, it's almost always necessary. It's okay to bond with total strangers over this stuff. They won't be strangers for long. As McKowen put it so perfectly in her first book,

> "One stranger who understands your experiences exactly will do for you what hundreds of close friends and family who don't understand cannot." [5]

My wife is pretty good about understanding that there are people out there who get it when she doesn't, and that I need those people. I need those relationships, those connections. Your spouse can't be (and shouldn't be) your sole source of support in every aspect of your life. They call it a support *system* for a reason, right? Beth is okay with me texting and talking to these people she's never met (some of them women). That in and of itself is a form of support.

I shudder to think where I would be on this journey without these folks. I'm pretty sure I still would be sober—but I think I would just be getting along. I wouldn't be as fulfilled. I wouldn't have learned as much along the way. I'm not sure I would love this sober life as much as I do. Shared experiences can be incredibly powerful, especially the whole "experience" of struggling with alcohol, because it involves such a significant life change. You're giving up something you've known and relied on for decades, but then there's the unbelievable payoff that you hadn't even known existed. To experience that by yourself is pure magic. When you do it with others or you can share it with others who understand, well, that's soul-shifting.

As for me and Beth, we made it through our own little storm. There was no magic moment when things turned around. There wasn't a spectacular blow-out fight that sparked a change (plenty of less spectacular little ones, though!). We just stayed with it and kept working. I got more comfortable in my sober skin. The Storm, after flexing its muscles for a couple of months, eventually quieted. I worked through the grieving process of losing my "friend" of 25 years. Those things by themselves went a long way toward resolving the issues with Beth.

I gained a deeper understanding of how Beth expresses support, and she became more receptive to how I receive it. She realized that our social life was going to survive, and I made more of an effort to meet her halfway on the things she still enjoyed doing. Beth started to see how sobriety was changing me for the better and started appreciating it more. I felt like she started to "get it." She began telling people how much happier I was. That meant a lot to me. It was affirmation that the changes I felt on the inside were visible to the rest of the world. She started telling the kids about me meeting with other people to talk about their alcohol issues. That made me feel like she was proud of me. In the end, we both got more comfortable with my sobriety.

Near the end of the process of writing this book, I took a trip to the Colorado mountains to be by myself, to just write for a few days without the distractions of work and home. When I unpacked my suitcase, I found a card from Beth. She wrote:

"I'm so proud of you for finishing this book and sharing your story. I know you will inspire so many people and they will learn so much from your story. Can't wait to read it!"

We've come a long way from giving up pizza.

CHAPTER SEVENTEEN

Magic Moments and Memorable Mornings

The Storm could have done me in. I easily could have given up. I could have decided that the loneliness, awkwardness, and annoyance of not drinking in a world where EVERYTHING centers around drinking was simply too much of a pain in the ass. I could have decided that it simply wasn't worth it.

But I didn't. I decided it was worth it. It was impossible for me to grasp at the time just how worth it it was. While the "never again" resolve that I vowed to hang onto after the weekend in Arizona was enough to power me forward all by itself early on, the glimpses of magic that I experienced ended up sustaining me in the longer run. There was just enough magic in the beginning—my friend dozing off on the couch, the LA trip with Beth and Landon, the NYC trip with my buddies—to help me weather the Storm. Then, little by little, more moments started happening. This sobriety thing kept showing itself to me, in ways big and small. With each moment, it became harder and harder to run from this new truth that I was discovering: life was better sober.

Four months after I quit, I took our daughter to Houston to watch the women's U.S. National Soccer Team play and to visit our old neighbors, who had moved there a couple years prior. They have three daughters, one of whom is Scarlett's age, and Scarlett had played with her a lot when we were neighbors. My not drinking was so new at this point, I hadn't yet decided whether I was giving it up for good. My friend and former neighbor was very supportive, so I didn't have to worry about dealing with that. Still, traveling, attending a sporting event, enjoying nice weather (coming from Omaha in February), hanging out with friends I hadn't seen in a while—there were a lot of things that I wasn't used to doing without alcohol.

Over all, the trip was great, and I loved being sober for it. It had the usual benefits that I was becoming used to and beginning to love so much. But there are two specific memories from that trip that I'll cherish for the rest of my days. Before the soccer match, Scarlett and I went to one of those places with bowling and arcade games. This was a nice place, with a full bar. We played ping-pong and skee ball and we bowled. I didn't have any burning desire to drink while we were there, but the fact that I wasn't drinking was on my mind constantly.

What I remember most about being there with Scarlett was noticing how much fun she was having. Not just making a passing mental note of it in my head, but stopping, observing, and soaking in how much fun she was having and how much fun I was having with her. This was something new to me. I almost always had fun with my kids during outings like this, but this was a different level. I was just more *there*. It was like I was the kid experiencing all this for the first time. It was joy on a level I hadn't experienced before. I wasn't thinking about the next drink I was going to order or how many I could have before we had to leave or before Scarlett would notice that I was starting to act differently. I could just be. It was so fulfilling. Not drinking elevated the experience, when I'd thought it would do the opposite.

Josh Brolin said:

> "Sobriety is a moment of being able to love and be consumed by the glee it brings someone else." [6]

That was my day with Scarlett.

***

The other memory that sticks out from that trip is from later that night in the hotel room. We came back after the game and got ready for bed. We lay in bed and talked about the game and our day. She put her head on my chest and said she wanted to snuggle. I love snuggling with my kids more than anything in the world. At that time, my boys were old enough that we didn't do it anymore, so Scarlett was my last snuggler. We just lay there for a while and talked. I don't even remember what we talked about. I just remember thinking that I never wanted to forget that moment. We snuggled the whole night. We still talk about that night sometimes. It brings tears to my eyes just thinking about it today.

Had I been drinking, I almost certainly would've had a beer sitting on the nightstand next to the bed. I don't even know that I would have been in the bed with Scarlett, because it would have been easier to drink sitting in a chair watching tv than lying in bed. I probably would have been content to give her an iPad while she lay in bed and I watched tv or stared at my phone while I tried to keep my buzz going from the game. Even if we still ended up snuggling, I would have been drunk and would have had nowhere near the appreciation for the moment that we ended up having. Not to mention it would have been different for Scarlett. And there's a good chance I would've drunk enough to wake up the next morning with some measure of guilt and shame—not to mention a hangover.

Experiencing those two moments sober was the beginning of me realizing that the moments that happen in sobriety—you know, *life*—can be profoundly more meaningful than what happens when I drink. The drinking versions of those two events would have been fine, but they would have been ordinary. They would have been what I was used to. The sober versions of those two events were life in living color. Those two moments—experiencing, *feeling* Scarlett's unbridled joy at playing ping-pong and bowling, being present as the two of us snuggled in bed with her head on my shoulder, and wishing the moment would never end—that's living life. The drinking version of those moments is just observing. You're just along for the ride. It's not *feeling*, it's not *being*, it's not *living*. Once you get a taste of that, it's impossible to tell yourself that drinking is worth it. How do I choose drinking over a night of snuggling with my daughter? How do I choose drinking over being fully immersed in her joy during bowling and arcade games? Those moments are what life is all about! Those are what I'm going to remember when I'm old. Not the empty pint glass that would have been sitting on the bedside table the next morning.

***

Around this time I kept coming back to the Orlando lawyer's comment. It was as if he'd given me permission to quit. I could see myself in him, and as I got further out from my last drink the true impact of him telling me his story was coming into focus.

Four months after I quit, I sent him an email:

> Peter, this is a personal note. I decided to stop drinking last October. I won't bore you with the details of my own personal journey, but there were several nudges I received along the way that ultimately got me to the decision to give up alcohol. One of those was when you mentioned during our mediation last summer that you decided to stop drinking when your oldest became a teenager. It probably didn't seem like anything to you at the time, but as I think back, I realize it was one of the many things that helped me make the leap to give up alcohol. So I just wanted to drop you a note to let you know that, and say thanks for mentioning it. You never know when your own story is going to have an impact on someone else!
>
> Not to say I don't crave a drink now and then, but I am really enjoying life without alcohol and have no doubt that it was one of the best decisions I've ever made.

Peter responded right away:

> Todd—You just made my day. Heck—my month. It gets easier and easier as time passes. At this point (over 4 years now), I can't imagine a circumstance that would cause me to go back. I'm really happy for you.

***

The first Christmas after I quit, my parents gave our kids some money but told them they had to use it to pay it forward somehow. I love these types of things that get our kids thinking about helping other people.

133

Scarlett, who was eight years old at the time, was so excited, and she started thinking right away about how to use the money. After bouncing a few ideas around, she decided to put together some "gift bags" for homeless people. I don't know where she got this idea—probably off TikTok—but I was all for it. So off we went to Target to buy the supplies. She put the bags together that night. Then they sat around our house for two months.

One Saturday in March, we were going to have a couple hours to kill between basketball games, and it didn't make sense for us to drive home, then back to the next game. We decided to take the bags with us and try to find somewhere to hand them out between the games.

After the first game, a group of parents went to a bar to eat and have some drinks. Normally, this would have been the part of the day I'd look forward to as much as, if not more than, the actual games. Beers in between games would have helped get me through the day. But after we ate, my daughter was chompin' at the bit to distribute the bags. So I took her and a couple of her teammates to go find some homeless people. Frankly, I was happy to do that instead of hanging out at the restaurant with people I didn't know all that well while I was not drinking. That was exactly the type of situation in which I would have leaned on the alcohol to ease the awkwardness.

We drove around downtown Omaha for a few minutes but didn't see any homeless people. I don't know exactly where I was going or what I expected to find. I felt like saying, "Hey, Siri, give me directions to the homeless people in Omaha." Usually there were scattered homeless people on a couple designated corners in certain parts of the downtown. But on that day it was pretty quiet. We saw one man walking down the street who we thought might be homeless, but we weren't sure. We didn't want to get out and offer him a gift bag if he wasn't. It was actually pretty funny to hear the girls debate whether or not he was homeless. One of them thought his shoes looked too new to be homeless. We decided to pass on him out of an abundance of caution.

I looked up the nearest homeless shelter, which was about five minutes away. As we pulled up to the building, there must have been a hundred people milling around outside. Various groups congregated in different spots outside the front door and on the front lawn. It reminded me of a middle school that had just gotten out for the day, if a bunch of homeless people went to that school. There were even more people scattered around the parking lot, almost like a tailgate scene but without the fired-up grills and festive backdrop. Some people were wandering around by themselves, some were talking to each other.

We parked on the side of the street that led to the parking lot and main entrance. You could sense that everyone knew some "outsiders" were approaching. The homeless folks were so eager for conversation and interaction. Everyone wanted to talk to the girls. At first, the homeless people didn't know what we were there for; they just wanted to talk. Have you ever visited family or loved ones in an assisted-living or old folks home? I'm always struck by how excited the residents are to see new faces. It's nice to bring them a couple of minutes of happiness by just engaging in conversation. I've also found it to be a little sad. That's what the homeless people's reaction reminded me of.

A couple of the girls were hesitant to walk toward the homeless people., but once one of the girls took the lead, they followed. The people we gave the bags to were so appreciative. They gushed with gratitude before they even knew what was in the bag. Their faces lit up. One woman hauling all her belongings in a grocery cart even cried. It stopped me in my tracks. The girls were the stars. They had their basketball uniforms on, so they got lots of questions about their team, where they were playing, and basketball in general. The girls, shy and timid at first, warmed up quickly, and their confidence grew. Soon they were handing out the bags without any direction or assistance from me. It was neat to watch.

We could have handed out five times as many gift bags as we had that day. It didn't take long before we were done handing out everything we had. A lot of people wanted to talk to the girls anyway, so we hung out for a few minutes after we were done. The girls were all smiles. So was I. They were bouncing as we walked back to the car. They talked about the experience during the entire ride back to the restaurant. Their faces were lit up. They wanted to make more bags and do it all over again. It was so neat to see them realize the value of service and compassion. Can you ask for anything more as a parent? It filled me up! Every time I think about it, it makes me smile. Before we got out of the car, one of the girls said, "That felt good."

Had I been drinking at the restaurant with the rest of the group, I would have lobbied hard for my wife to take my daughter instead, or I would have been more than willing to let some other parent fall on the sword. If I had taken her, I would have been resentful about having to give up some of my drinking time to do so. That resentment would have intruded on the entire experience. I would have started off the excursion pissed that I had to do it. And what would I have been missing? Sitting at a sports bar with people I didn't know very well just so I could drink beer? What a shame that would've been! I would have viewed the experience as something just to "get through" instead of something to actually *experience*. I wouldn't have shown up for it. I would have missed out. And, lo and behold, it was easily the highlight of my weekend, and something I'll remember and smile about for a long time. I hope the girls will too. That beats drinking any day.

***

About eight months after I quit, I played in a member-guest golf tournament. If you're not familiar with those events, they're always big drinking affairs. This one is no exception. It's held at a nice golf resort in the middle of Nebraska, so everyone there was staying on site, not going home at the end of the day, and were without kids. That makes it an even bigger party than most member-guests.

I did a lot of thinking about whether I wanted to go on the trip at all. I didn't want to accept the invite if I didn't think I was going to have a good time. My wife wanted to go but would have been fine if I'd decided not to. I had been to this member-guest before, when I was drinking, and I'd had a lot of fun. I knew what I was in for. The member who invited me is a big drinker, and I worried that he would end up regretting he'd invited me. I was actually a little surprised that he had invited me, since he knew that I didn't drink anymore. I just wanted to make sure that I could enjoy it at this point in my sobriety. Finally, I decided that I could. I figured, the resort is great, the golf itself is fantastic, and there are some really fun "regulars." Plus, I figured it would be a chance to spend some time with my wife away from the kids. So I accepted the invite.

Each night after the golf, there is a dinner and a big party at the club-house. At this member-guest, that usually means live music on the patio that overlooks a very scenic part of the property. There's a massive fire pit. Everywhere you look, the backdrop is gorgeous. The food is fantastic. It's a wonderful setting. All this makes overdoing it pretty easy. A lot of the people there had been drinking for most of the day during the golf, so everyone was already in party mode. I stayed for the dinner, but not long afterward (when the party started really picking up), I was ready to retire to the cabin.

I spent a *lot* of time planning my exit. I was convinced that as soon as I made a move for the door, the lead singer of the band would stop the music and turn toward me. Then a spotlight would shine down from the sky right on my face, and he would ask me to explain myself, while every one of the three hundred guests looked on. But the music didn't stop as I left. Nobody even noticed. As I walked down the dark gravel road to our cabin, I was happy to be retreating to the solitude of the cabin. Yes, I had a twinge of FOMO and felt guilt for leaving my friend, his wife, and my wife. But the FOMO was gone by the time I climbed into bed.

Had I run my Race to Nowhere that whole day and evening, the following morning would have been dicey. Physically, the best-case scenario would have been a slight headache and general fogginess. The worst-case scenario would have been a splitting headache, nausea, and an inability to string complete sentences together. Oh, and pile on top of that regret, shame, and embarrassment for drinking too much and not handling my alcohol. Being concerned that people were talking about me. Beating myself up for not keeping things under control (again). Regardless, I wouldn't have been feeling great.

As I walked into the clubhouse for breakfast, every time I passed someone or saw somebody across the room, my mind immediately would have started racing:

> Did I meet him for the first time last night?
> Did I talk to him last night?
> What did we talk about?
> Did I say something stupid?

There would be the customary, "Wow, things got out of hand quickly last night!" comments, and all of us would laugh. I would raise my eyebrows and say something like "You're not kidding!" and act like everything was normal. Meanwhile, on the inside I simultaneously would be scrambling to piece together the night before and trying to suppress the feeling that I hated this exercise so much. It never sucked less, no matter how many times I'd done it before.

I would be convinced that every person I saw that morning was thinking to himself or herself, "Holy shit, that guy was wasted last night." I would be in a hurry to get out of there so we could move on to the next day of drinking. That approach sort of felt like a reset of the night before, that we were putting it in the rearview mirror. What never seemed to register with me was that I simply was starting the cycle all over again.

In contrast, on that actual next morning—the one that *didn't* follow a Race to Nowhere—I got up early, went to the gym, went back to our cabin to shower and dress for golf, and then headed back up to the clubhouse for breakfast. My "ordinary" walk into the clubhouse became something I didn't expect. It hit me out of nowhere, and it did so with a force that I still think about it today, because it made me feel so good. I swung open the giant, heavy, wooden door and started walking through the main room. At that moment, I realized that I didn't have a care in the world about the previous night. No piecing it together. No wondering whether I'd had an awkward conversation with someone. No worrying whether I needed to apologize for anything. None of that! I felt fucking seven feet tall walking through that clubhouse. Like I was walking on air, like I owned the world. And to top it all off, I felt great physically. I was fresh, I'd gotten in a workout, and I had no trouble stringing together complete sentences.

Knowing how much I loved sober mornings, I'd known I would feel good that first morning. But this was different—this was even better than I was expecting. It stopped me in my tracks. It jolted me enough that I told myself to pause and take notice of how fucking good it felt. It was like the run in Central Park a month after I quit. I wanted to bottle the feeling and remember it forever. If I could do that, there was no way I ever would drink again. Well, I didn't bottle it, but I still remember it. I still smile when I think about it. I'm still incredibly grateful for the moment.

All the awkwardness that comes with getting sober, all the worrying about what people will think, all the feeling like you're an outcast, all the mourning over losing a best friend, all the shit that comes with quitting— none of that is any fun. But when I stacked it up against the feeling I had that morning in that clubhouse, all the bad stuff felt so much smaller. All the bad stuff felt soooo worth it. I wanted the feeling from that morning more than I wanted what came with drinking. It wasn't even close.

And here's the thing: You can't have those moments if you don't give up drinking for a while. You don't have to commit to giving it up forever. But to experience things like a morning that makes you feel like a million bucks, you do have to give it up for some amount of time (longer than a weekend—sorry). You have to open yourself up and allow yourself to feel these things. The only way to do that is to remove alcohol from your life for some significant period. I didn't know these feelings were even a thing, and I never would have known they were possible if I hadn't given up alcohol. Once I got a taste of how good it felt to walk into that clubhouse after not drinking the night before, I wanted more. When you're quitting, first you have to learn how to live without it. Then you learn how to LIVE without it. I was learning how to LIVE.

CHAPTER EIGHTEEN

The Other Side

October 20, 2021, marked my one-year anniversary of giving up alcohol. I was a little surprised at how special the day was. I felt like I had crossed some sort of rubicon, like I had made it to the other side, like a graduation of sorts—even if I didn't know exactly what the next phase looked like. But I was ready for it. I was ready to take on the world as a nondrinker. I was very proud of myself for making it through one year.

Around my one-year anniversary, I felt a strong pull to help people. Along with my strong feeling of accomplishment, I was immensely grateful for everything and everyone who had helped get me there. Every story I heard, every conversation I had, every book I read had helped so much. I took something from all of it. I wanted to help people in a way similar to how and how much I'd been helped. That's where the idea for this book was born.

I also decided to "come out" on social media. It was not a secret to anyone close to me that I'd given up drinking, but, partly because of COVID, a lot of my friends and acquaintances didn't know. But the day before I came out, while I was mowing the lawn (when I do some of my best thinking), some doubts began to creep in about whether I should post anything about my issues with alcohol.

What will people think?

What if it hurts me professionally?

Are people going to think I was a deadbeat who drank every day in secret?

Are they going to wonder what kind of parent I've been?

Are they going to think it got really bad?

Then I turned it around. I thought about Laura McKowen, who so courageously told her story in *We Are the Luckiest*. I thought about what a huge help her book had been to me. I recalled how reading it had been one of the first times I got genuinely excited about the prospect of a life without alcohol. Her book gave me hope. It reinforced that I was making the right decision and was on the right path. It also gave me permission to be pissed sometimes about giving up alcohol and to know that it was okay to feel like that. That played as big a part in getting me through the Storm as anything.

So, when those doubts started creeping in about making my story public and I was worried about what people would think about me, I said to myself, "Well, how do you feel about Laura McKowen?"

"I respect the shit out of her and I admire her bravery."

"Well then, post your damn story on social media and stop coming up with excuses why you shouldn't."

So I did. After summarizing my journey, I concluded with the following:

> I want to put this out there for anyone who has thought about giving up drinking or is trying to give it up. Whether it's been a fleeting thought or something that keeps nagging at you over time (like it did for me), if you want someone to talk to, please feel free to reach out to me. Send me a private message. The conversations I have had with people who gave up drinking are immensely valuable to me. I don't know if I would have decided to stop drinking without some of those conversations. The ones I've had since I quit have been helpful beyond words. So please reach out if you're so inclined. I actually love talking about this stuff.

It was scary putting that out there—I almost talked myself out of it at the last minute. I read and reread the post several times. Does that sentence sound weird? Are people going to understand what I'm trying to say here? My finger hovered over the "post" button for what seemed like thirty seconds.

I'm glad I didn't chicken out. I absolutely was blown away by the responses I received. Not just the notes of support, which felt really good, but the number of people who reached out to me to share their own stories or the stories of loved ones was incredible. It was the same discovery I'd made when I joined TLC: There are so many people out there struggling with the same or similar alcohol issues, yet we all think we're the only ones and there's nobody to talk to about it. I ended up meeting with several people, some of them regularly, to talk about their desire to quit or a family member's issues with alcohol. From that Facebook post, I made connections that I still carry on today.

I also shared my story in a TLC meeting around my one-year anniversary. Bolstered by the incredible response I'd received to my Facebook post, I was excited to share my story "in person" on the Zoom TLC meeting. But I was still nervous because I didn't think my story was interesting enough. There was no rock bottom involving the police, no car crash. No waking up in an alley. No stint in rehab. No court battle for custody of my kids that scared me straight. Just a normal, boring dude who couldn't figure out how to drink normally, so he gave it up. The host of the meeting knew about my reservations. As she was introducing me, she read a passage that so perfectly addressed my fears. The main point of the passage essentially was that everyone's story is worth telling, and everyone's story has value to someone else. It was exactly what I needed to hear.

Sharing my story turned out to be one of the best things I've ever done. The feedback I received is something I'll remember for a long time. But more than that, it led to some of the connections I'm most grateful for today. I learned something first hand from these two experiences: Good things happen when we share our stories. Even the parts that make us cringe—especially those! People gravitate to people who are being vulnerable and honest. We are starved for those two things in our social media–obsessed world, which so often promotes carefully curated and staged perfection that is hardly ever real or genuine.

Something crystalized for me at the one-year mark. A wave washed over me made up of gratitude, peace, happiness, and awe. I had made it through to the other side. The Storm had passed. The sky opened up and I could see clearly again. I loved what I saw, I loved what I felt. I was blown away by it all, partly because it felt so good and partly because I didn't see most of it coming. October 20 now means more to me than my birthday.

When I started this journey, I thought life without alcohol would be fine. I knew there would be positives. I knew I would feel better physically, and I knew that I would feel better about myself. I thought it would really suck to give it up but, on balance, life overall probably would be marginally better.

I also thought that I would miss alcohol every single day for the rest of my life. I thought I would carry around this nagging feeling that I was missing out on something—a perpetual case of FOMO. A twinge of regret that never fully dissipated, no matter how good for me it was to give it up. I envisioned this internal back and forth for the rest of my life, where I was burdened with the lure of alcohol and all the fun that came with it and the need to tamp it down by reminding myself that life was better without it. I thought it would be a lifelong struggle that would ease over time but never fully dissipate. I thought the Storm, while maybe varying in intensity, always would be there in some form.

I was wrong about all of that. I can tell you that sobriety is far beyond marginally better than my drinking life. I no longer miss alcohol. My bouts of FOMO have been replaced with gratitude about my new sober life. If someone had told me this when I was considering giving up alcohol, I would have bet a very large sum of money that the person was full of shit. "Oh, come on, it can't be that much better. That's impossible!" I would have been 100% certain of that. I had no clue about what awaited me. I didn't know what I didn't know. I can't tell you how much it blows my mind that I enjoy life so much more without alcohol than I did when I drank. Part of that is because it's just impossible to *truly* appreciate the blessings of sobriety without experiencing them yourself. If you're skeptical, I was too. It's been such an unexpected blessing for me that I was inspired to write a book about it.

Stupid happiness. That's what sobriety feels like at times. Brought on by something as small as a car ride with your son, a sunrise, a fight that didn't happen, or a smile from your daughter. Life's little things just hit differently.

I don't mean that your life simply and magically gets better the moment you give up alcohol. Your other problems don't disappear. Life still happens. You still have the stress of work. You still worry about your kids and wonder whether you're doing anything right as a parent. You still feel that sometimes there's not enough time in the day to get everything done.

But while life itself still happens, dealing with life is much better. It's easier, it's lighter, it's calmer. The best way I can sum it up is like this: There's more of the good stuff and less of the bad. There's more peace, less anxiety. More connection, less distance. More presence, less distraction. More self-esteem, less shame and regret. More honesty, less deception. More calm, less chaos. More feeling, less numbing. More confidence, less self-doubt. More clarity, less fogginess. There's more gratitude—so much more gratitude. I thought I was a grateful person before I stopped drinking, but the amount of gratitude I felt before can't even compare to now. Above all, there's more living, less escaping, less just getting through the day. It's been amazing, invigorating, and unexpected. It's a life I never knew was out there.

There's a saying: "I got sober because I wanted a better life. I stay sober because I got one." I can't describe it any better than that.

CHAPTER NINETEEN

Parenting Sober

"Sobriety is when your kids can look at you and trust what they see." [7]

I feel like I was born to be a few things, and a dad is one of them. I think it's the greatest gig in the world. It's also the hardest. Nobody knows how to do it perfectly, and if anyone tells you they have all the answers they're full of shit. Parenting is 50% worrying and wondering what the right thing to do is, 25% putting into action whatever you think the right thing to do is, and 25% crossing your fingers hoping you're doing something right. It's a lot of trial and error. It's a lot of beating yourself up for not always knowing the answer. It's a lot of hoping and praying.

The thing about parenting is, there's very little real-time feedback on whether you're doing anything right. Wouldn't it be nice if your kid would come to you and say, "You know, Dad, I know it was really hard for you to ground me for sneaking out, but you did the right thing, and it'll have a positive impact on me going forward." Or wouldn't it help if you could peer into the future and see—during those moments when your teenager is grunting one-word answers to your questions while staring at his phone—that he'll turn out to be a productive member of society?

As much as I've always enjoyed being a dad, it's even better sober. The improvement in my parenting, my relationship with my kids, and just my

145

general approach to them is easily one of my favorite things about getting sober. Like most of the gifts that sobriety bestows, this one didn't present as a drastic, sudden change that hit me like a bolt of lightning. It's been gradual and mostly subtle. It's a gift that keeps on giving and will continue to show up for me as I get older and they get older. There are still challenges, but—like so much in life when you get sober—they're easier to manage. And I'm so much more confident in my ability to manage them.

My kids didn't suddenly start listening to me and doing everything I say. They didn't start waking up on Saturday morning asking how they could help around the house. They didn't start picking up their rooms. They sure as hell didn't stop leaving wrappers and dirty dishes all over the house. And they certainly didn't stop farting or sniping at each other. But here's what did happen: I started listening to them more. I started observing them more. I started *being there* for them more. I stopped reacting and started responding. The overall mindfulness and sense of peace that comes with sobriety probably shows up in my parenting more than any other area of my life.

***

At nine months sober, on a random weeknight in the summer, I had a parenting moment that never would have happened if I'd been drinking. We were invited over to some friends' house to grill and eat dinner. Our kids are friends with their kids, and they always enjoy hanging out together. This couple likes to drink, and when I was drinking with them I knew my glass always would be full. The guy himself was one of those guys who never said no when asked, "Want one more?" He's one of those guys who fills your glass before you're even done. When I was drinking, I thought this was awesome. It was a way to drink more without taking full responsibility. "I didn't even want that much wine, but Chris kept pouring me more!" I never wanted to say no anyway, but it was even better if I could pass on the responsibility for saying yes to someone else.

That night at our friends' was uneventful. We sat around and talked, everyone but me had some drinks, we grilled out, and then we went home. Had I been drinking, I'm 99% sure I would have come home with a good buzz, at a minimum. It was a nice summer night, we were sitting outside, we didn't have anything to rush off to. The ingredients were there. And, let's be honest, I didn't need all those ingredients anyway to get a good buzz on.

We got home around 9:30 pm. Beth and Austin got into an argument—I don't even remember what about. Austin was just generally acting like an asshole, and he was pretty disrespectful to Beth. Their argument ended with him stomping off to his bedroom downstairs and my wife going upstairs to our room. I marched downstairs to let Austin know that talking to his mom like that was not acceptable, then went back up to our bedroom.

Had I been drinking, that would have been the end of our interaction for the night. I was tired as it was, but if I had drunk at our friends' house, I would have been even more tired and sapped of any motivation to do anything other than go to bed. I had done by my fatherly and husbandly duty by sticking up for my wife, and I would have considered my job done.

But this time when I got back up to our bedroom, my therapist's words popped into my head—and they began pulling me back downstairs. "Show him some grace," she always would say. "Show him some compassion." I stopped fixating on the ugly words that had come out of Austin's mouth toward Beth and started thinking that something probably was bothering him. In this way, kids aren't any different from adults. More often than not, the conflicts we get into aren't over the issue we think we're fighting about. When I get mad about the thirty-fourth cereal bowl that gets left on the counter instead of put into the dishwasher, I'm usually not mad about the cereal bowl itself (okay, sometimes I am—not the best example). Our fights with our loved ones usually are about something beneath the surface, not the issue of the moment that we think we're fighting over. My son wasn't upset over whatever he and Beth were fighting about. Through the fight, he simply was expressing his angst about other things. In hindsight, it was so obvious that something else was going on. In the moment, though, when he's being disrespectful to his mom, that can be hard to see.

I went back downstairs and asked what was bothering him. We ended up talking for about forty-five minutes. He told me about some pretty heavy stuff that was going on—things I'd had no idea about. I spent much of the conversation trying to figure out what to say and how to comfort him. I think I failed miserably at this. As my therapist told me later, "You don't have to come up with the perfect response. It doesn't have to be perfect." I listened a lot. I tried to think of things to say that would provide him with comfort. More than anything, I wanted him to know that I was there for him and I loved him. So, we hugged, we cried, I told him I loved him, and I let him know that we would talk some more.

I left the conversation feeling anxious about what was bothering him, but also very thankful that I'd had the mindfulness to absorb and listen to my therapist's words. That Austin was able to express his feelings to me and I was able to be there to hear him and hug him and tell him it was going to be okay is something I will be grateful for forever. When you boil this parenting stuff down to its simplest form, that's what it's all about: communicating, being there for your kids, and making your kids feel safe and comfortable enough to tell you about feelings they're struggling with. And then talking that stuff out, helping them to navigate those things and figure out a way through. If we can do that for our kids, the chances that they'll grow up to be happy, emotionally healthy adults go way up. The grades, the accolades, the athletic achievements—all that is so small, so insignificant compared with providing our kids with the tools to navigate life in a healthy manner.

The drinking me never would have discovered what was bothering Austin. I don't know what, if anything, would have happened if we hadn't had that conversation. Maybe nothing. But maybe something bad. Maybe his feelings would have stayed bottled up inside. Maybe he would have continued to lash out. Maybe he would have found an unproductive and dangerous way to let it all out. He still might, of course. But maybe that conversation leads to another one down the road. Maybe he remembers that time we talked the next time he's struggling with something. Maybe he remembers the hug we shared. That conversation was an important building block for us, a building block that never would have happened had I been drinking that night. The gift that sobriety gave me that night is something I won't soon forget.

***

When I was almost two years sober, Austin got into his second car accident within ten days. He had been sixteen for less than a month. The first one was a one-car accident. Someone turned in front of him, and he panicked and drove up onto a curb, which happened to be covered by a sewer. The accident did ten thousand dollars' worth of damage to his car. Of course.

Nine days later—while his car was still in the shop!—he took Beth's car to pick up Landon at a friend's house. About a minute after he left, I got a call from him. He was clearly panicked. He was half crying, half hyper-ventilating.

"Dad. Dad!"

"What?"

"I hit someone!"

At this point, I was thinking he might have hit a pedestrian. I was scared shitless.

"You hit someone in their car?"

"Yes."

Momentary relief.

"Is everyone okay?"

"Yes. There's damage to his car. Mom's car is fine."

More relief.

"Okay, okay. Hold on. It's okay. I'll be right there. Just hang tight. I'll be right there."

When I got to the scene, Austin was barely holding back tears.

"I don't even want to drive anymore!" he said, no longer holding back those tears.

The entire left side of his body was shaking. I put my hand on his shoulder, then I gave him a hug. He was still shaking. The guy he hit couldn't have been nicer. He wasn't mad, he was calm. He was so kind to Austin. I'll never forget that. And I promise you, if I'm ever in an accident with a teenager and it's the teenager's fault, I'll be as kind to that teenager as this guy was to Austin. When we exchanged texts later, I thanked him for the way he'd handled it. The guy responded that Austin was a good kid, and we should be proud of how he'd handled himself.

Between when I hung up the phone and when I met up with Austin, part of me was pissed as hell. "Are you fucking kidding me? ANOTHER accident?! We're going to be uninsurable! How do you get in two accidents in nine days?! Your car is still in the shop from your last accident! Do you

need to spend a year taking driver's ed?! What the fuck? HOW DOES
THIS HAPPEN?!?!"

All those thoughts raged through my head. But I collected myself
while I drove over to meet him. When I got to the scene, he was so shaken
up that I don't know how any parent could have yelled at their kid in that
moment. When it was time to drive home, I didn't think Austin was
collected enough to drive (no need for accident number three!), so I drove
him and left my car there. Before we went home, I texted Beth to let her
know how rattled he was and to make sure she didn't verbalize any of the
inner thoughts I was having or that she might be having. She met him in
the driveway and gave him a hug.

I was so, so grateful for the way we handled this. I was damn proud
of us. I was proud of myself! I know that I handled the incident differently as a sober parent than I would have if I'd been drinking. For one, I
almost certainly would have had some drinks in me that day when the
call came in from Austin. That afternoon, I'd watched a soccer game on
tv (previously a drinking activity), then went to the pool for a little while
(another drinking activity) before going to the grocery store. I came
home and was getting ready to grill (definitely a drinking activity) when
I got the call from Austin. So that alone would've affected my reaction to
the situation.

But beyond that, being sober for 20 months when this happened
helped me be mindful about staying calm and "being there" for Austin
instead of yelling at him. I was calmer—at least on the outside! I wasn't
nearly as reactive as I would have been when I was drinking. I was reflec-
tive, and I took time to take a breath and think before I simply let my
inner thoughts take over. I'd never done this when I was drinking.
Sobriety is a gift that shows up in big ways and in small ways. That day, it
showed up in a big way for me and my son.

The talk with Austin after our night out at our friends' and the
second accident in nine days were bigger moments. But the inner peace
I have now shows up every single day in much smaller, but equally
important, ways. My newfound calm has reduced the number of stupid,
unnecessary arguments with my teenage kids by about 90%. I'm so much
less reactive than I used to be. If you're familiar with teenagers, you know

that during the course of a day they can say approximately 47 things that make you think some version of, "Are you fucking kidding me?" Those types of comments used to set me off and lead to dumb, petty arguments with my kids. They don't anymore.

The morning Austin was to take the ACT, he made one of those comments. Instead of responding out loud with "are you fucking kidding me?," I just stood there and said nothing. I let it go. I didn't push back. We moved on and had a conversation about something else. After he left the house, I was so grateful that he didn't drive off to school to take the ACT just after having a fight with me.

***

In addition to being a calmer dad, I'm also more available to my kids now. Looking back, my drinking affected my availability to my kids in ways that I didn't even grasp. I see it now with some of my kids' friends' parents. The majority of my drinking took place on weekend nights. Sometimes at home, sometimes out with other families, including kids, and sometimes out with adults only. Regardless, I think my kids had come to expect that on typical Friday and Saturday nights I would be drinking, and that that would be my main focus for the night. This may have been only at a subconscious level. But I think what happens when kids get to that point is, they shut down during those times as far as you're concerned. You're off the clock, and they know it. You're not available to them—truly available—and they sense that too. That unavailability can stretch into the next day when you're hung over or just generally sluggish. All that takes its toll, on them individually and on your relationship with them. You're saying to them: "I won't be available to you as a parent from 8 pm on tonight." (This happens with spouses too, which is a whole separate conversation.)

It may seem like a small thing, and you may be thinking to yourself, "I'm an adult who works hard and does a lot for my kids. I deserve some time to myself!" That's what I told myself for years. And we do all deserve time to ourselves. We're better parents (and spouses) when we are in a good place mentally and taking care of ourselves. But regularly checking out because you're prioritizing alcohol over your family, which is what I was doing, isn't exactly self-care. It takes its toll and sends a message to your kids. It creates distance and builds resentment. Kids stop looking at you as someone they can count on.

So, is checking out for a couple hours on the weekend that big of a deal? In a vacuum, it doesn't seem like much. But when it's every weekend, or more, then before you know it your kids just assume you won't be available to them. You won't be *there* as a mom or dad. The Great Intruder will be there instead. So then, *they* start to check out. And honestly, sometimes it's easier when they check out and just accept that you won't be there. The Great Intruder doesn't have competition. You can enjoy the drinking more, without the interference of parenting, of life. That's how I felt sometimes. Just let me drink in peace, please.

***

Mother's Day 2023 fell while I was in the middle of the 47th revision of this chapter. At that time, I was concerned that I didn't have any illustrative examples of my kids checking out because of my drinking because, well, when those incidents happened I'd been drinking, so I didn't notice. I know they happened, though—more times than I like to admit. Then, I happened upon a real-life example. It didn't involve me, but it easily could have a few years earlier.

We were at brunch with several other families. I got up to walk to the buffet at the same time as one of our kids' friends.

"Do you have big things planned for your mom today?" I asked the girl.

"No," she said, matter-of-factly.

"Oh, that's too bad," I replied.

"She's just going to drink mimosas all day anyway."

Her eyes betrayed her "I don't care" vibe that teens so often default to. They narrowed and pierced just enough that her contempt, which was just a shield to disguise her hurt and sadness, shone through.

Her comment took me by surprise, even though it probably shouldn't have. I wished her mom could have seen that look in her eyes and heard the pain in her voice. I just said "Oh . . ." and trailed off as we went to separate buffet lines. I felt like I should say something comforting, but I was blank. Her comment stuck with me the rest of that day, though. I felt sad for her and her mom.

***

At 9:30 pm on the 4th of July of my second year sober, Austin texted Beth and me, asking for someone to pick him up from a party. He was at a lake house and the kids had gone out to a nearby field and started lighting off some fireworks. He saw a woman in a home nearby who was watching them pretty closely. At one point, she got on her phone. Austin thought she was calling the cops, so he called for a ride home. He also wasn't entirely comfortable with the number of drunk adults at the party. "Let's just say they're not going to be sober by the end of the night," he told me when I picked him up.

Austin had called at the exact moment I was getting ready to sit down and watch a soccer game I'd been looking forward to all day. But I wasn't annoyed. We've told our kids over and over to call in these exact situations. This was the first time any of them had ever done it. He's doing exactly what we ask them to do, I told myself. This is a good thing! I was proud of him, and I told him that as soon as he got into the car. I told him again when we got home.

I shudder to think of what kind of shape I would've been in at 9:30 pm on the 4th of July just two years earlier. I wouldn't have been able to drive legally—I can guarantee you that. What would I have done? I either would have driven drunk, or I wouldn't even have been present enough to receive Austin's text and deal with it in any way. Either option is embarrassing. When you compare the sober outcome with what would have happened had I been drinking, how do you compete with sobriety?

***

Around my two-year-sober anniversary, I found myself on a party bus with about eight guys and some of our kids. It was an all-day affair. There were probably six or eight kids on the bus. I think the youngest was around nine, so it wasn't like they needed a lot of attention. But still, I watched as a couple of the guys just completely disappeared as dads. Their kids may as well have been on the bus without a parent.

153

At the end of the trip, one of the girls couldn't find her phone and was upset about it. Her dad was extremely drunk and of zero help to her. One other guy and I helped her look for it and eventually found it. I don't know whether her dad even knew what was going on. None of the guys (besides one) helped clean up the bus after we got back home. And then they drove their own cars home to their houses! With their kids inside! I took two kids home so they wouldn't drive with their very drunk dad, but I still cringe to this day that I didn't do more. Several inappropriate comments were made, some of which the kids heard and some they didn't. Overall, it was not a good environment for kids. The whole thing just felt gross to me.

I don't say any of this with judgment. Believe me, I would have been right there with everyone else not that long before. I would have laughed off the inappropriate comments. I would have checked out as a dad for most of the day. I would have been little to no help if my kid had lost his phone. I wouldn't have been too concerned with cleaning up the bus. And I almost certainly would have been legally drunk when it came time to drive my car and my kids home. Those dads didn't do anything I hadn't done myself or would have done that day if I was still drinking. I tell the story because, witnessing it all from a sober point of view, it blows my mind that I chose the drinking version for as long as I did. While I have some sadness about that, it's overridden by the gratitude I have now that I discovered a more fulfilling way.

***

On New Year's Eve when I was a little over three years sober, we were in Denver, celebrating with the Sullivans. We always spend New Year's together, alternating between Denver and Omaha. Between my siblings and the Sullivan girls, we have seventeen kids, ranging in age between four and seventeen. On this particular night, some of the kids were clamoring to go to Wal-Mart. I have no idea why. It was around 9 pm—why wouldn't you go to Wal-Mart at 9 pm on New Year's Eve? Because I'm not insane, I didn't take them, but while they were pleading their case, my nephew said, "Todd can drive us, he's the responsible one."

This particular night was probably the tamest New Year's Eve this group had ever had. Everyone was tired, a few of us weren't feeling well.

There wasn't much drinking going on. I don't remember anyone being drunk. Moreover, my nephew doesn't live in a house with a lot of drinking. And yet he turned to me as "the responsible one." That's another way to describe being available.

***

After an Iowa game during my second year sober, Scarlett and I were sitting at a table in the hotel lobby. She was making bracelets. Her brothers and cousin were at a nearby table eating and watching football. This was the time when I would've kicked my drinking up a notch, especially after a big win. I surveyed the lobby bar area, where most of the people were pretty drunk. At the table to my right, there was a boy who looked to be about ten or eleven sitting with his parents and friends. The adults looked like they had been at it for most of the day and were intent on keeping the party going. They were absent. They were me. The boy looked bored and distant. He was one of my kids.

Scarlett told me to close my eyes because she wanted to give me a bracelet she'd made for me. I closed my eyes and held out my wrist so she could put it on me. When I opened my eyes, I looked down and saw her creation. It said "Best Dad" on it. Sometimes I have moments when gratitude just washes over me. When I'm overwhelmed by how positive a change this has been for me and my life. When I feel a high that's hard to describe to people who haven't been on this journey. This was one of those moments. I've worn that bracelet every day since then.

Here were two tables. They were only a couple of feet apart, yet miles away from each other. I sat back, looked down at my new bracelet, and marveled at my journey from one table to the other.

***

A couple of weeks later, I took Scarlett and a friend to Iowa City for a football game. I was a little surprised at how excited she was for the trip. I loved it, but she normally wasn't that excited about football games. After we arrived, Scarlett and her friend ventured off on their own to look at the merchandise tents and find a shirt for Scarlett's friend. We tailgated for a bit, then headed off to the game.

Afterward, we went back to the hotel and the girls swam for a little bit. Then we decided to shower and go downtown for dinner and ice cream. This ended up being the best part of the trip. As we walked through the pedestrian mall, a bike taxi passed us and asked whether we wanted a ride. The girls really wanted to do it. We didn't need a ride anywhere—we were about a block or two away from where we were going to dinner. But I figured, what the hell, and we hopped on. Scarlett's face lit up. "I'm so excited!" she exclaimed. Shortly after we started going, she said, "This is sooo much fun!" Her smile was infectious and made my heart melt. As a parent, there's nothing better than seeing your kids unabashedly happy and excited about something.

We ditched the plans to eat at the restaurant and decided to eat outside because it was so nice out. Most of the restaurants in the ped mall have outdoor seating, and it was a perfect night to sit outside. We settled on a walking taco vendor because that's what the girls wanted. They sat on a bench and ate their walking tacos, then walked over to a playground across from the mall and played there while I ate my dinner. Then we went for ice cream.

After that—and this was the cherry on top for the girls—we went to Target. That's right, Target. We discovered that there was a Target in the ped mall, which seemed to mystify and excite the girls more than anything like that should mystify or excite anyone. The ped mall is the last place you'd expect to find a place like a Target. It's full of bars, restaurants, and shops, and most have apartments on the upper levels. It's the centerpiece of the social scene in Iowa City. Musicians hang out and play there. There are outdoor concerts. It's where people go for social interaction. It's one of the best things about Iowa City. It's also not where you'd expect to see a big-box store.

The girls begged to go inside. I gave up trying to understand why they were so excited about going to a store that they could go to at home anytime they wanted, and we went inside. Scarlett and her friend pretend-shopped for Scarlett's pretend-apartment. They had a blast. I stayed as long as I could, then stepped outside, sat at a table, and watched football on my phone while I fielded calls from Scarlett asking whether she could buy things. When the girls had satisfied their Target fix, we walked over to the

Old Capitol and took a couple of pictures. I ended up getting one of my all-time favorite photos: of Scarlett and me, with the Old Capitol in the background. Then we got in the car, drove back to the hotel, and sat outside by the fire pit and watched the end of the football game.

It was a fantastic night with my daughter and her friend. I got to see them smile countless times. They laughed. We had great conversations—especially over ice cream, when we talked about where they wanted to go to college and what they wanted to be in life. These moments with your kids—they don't happen every day. You blink and they go from six to twelve to eighteen and out the door. Scarlett is going to remember this trip. She's going to remember that bike-taxi ride. She's going to remember that Target. She's going to remember our picture by the Old Capitol.

That night never would have happened had I been drinking. Here's what most likely would have happened: When we got back to the hotel after the game, I would have had to resume drinking. I would have been focused on it, that's for sure. I wouldn't have drunk during the game, so I would be telling myself, "Okay, good job. Now it's time to start the party." I would've had a beer or two (probably two) while the girls swam. And then I wouldn't have wanted to go downtown because that would have involved driving, and that would have meant that I would have to watch my drinking more than I wanted to. I would've much preferred to stay at the hotel, where I could drink without the worry of driving, so I would've tried to convince Scarlett and her friend that it would be much more fun to just hang out at the hotel. Who knows, we might never have left the hotel that night.

But if we had made the trip downtown, I would've been preoccupied with:

1) drinking,
2) having to drive home.

I wouldn't have agreed to the bike taxi, because that would have delayed getting to the restaurant, where I could drink. I wouldn't have agreed to the taco stand, because I would've preferred a restaurant where we could sit down and I could order a beer. I wouldn't have enjoyed them playing on the playground because I would've been looking for a bar where I could drink but keep an eye on them at the same time. I wouldn't have

157

wanted to go for ice cream because that would mean waiting that much longer until we got back to the hotel, where I could drink again. And I certainly wouldn't have agreed to Target because—well, see the reason I wouldn't have agreed to ice cream. And even if I had agreed to all that, I would've been preoccupied with drinking instead of enjoying my time with the girls, just soaking it all in.

That night we had—it felt like living. I felt pure, Christmas-morning-as-a-kid joy. I have a picture of Scarlett on the bike taxi, and the smile on her face and the shine in her eyes bring a tear to my eye every time I look at it. That picture alone could keep me sober for the rest of my life.

The mind-blowing part is that I had no idea that all this was out there until I stopped drinking. Sure, I'd experienced lots of fun nights with my kids. We made lots of memories. I would have described my drinking self as someone who enjoyed life and made the most out of things. But this was different. It was elevated. It was life without the fog that I hadn't even known was there.

***

My kids were fourteen, twelve, eleven, and seven when I quit drinking. As kids enter adolescence, they need us parents more than ever. It's a hell of a time to be a kid. Their hormones are going crazy, their bodies are changing, they're having thoughts they've never had before. They're pushing boundaries, navigating peer pressure and other friend drama, and trying to find themselves. They want to grow up, but of course they're not grown up yet. It's more important than ever for us to be there for our kids during this time. We don't have to have all the answers (I hope to God we don't!). We don't have to always know the perfect thing to say. We don't have to fix all their problems—we can't and shouldn't fix all their problems. But we need to be there for them. We need to be reliable. We need to be present.

If you had asked me when I was drinking whether I was "present" for my kids, I would have said, "Absolutely." In my mind, I was. I was a pretty good dad, I think, when I was drinking. I showed up, I put in the time. But no matter how present I thought I was during my drinking days, I wasn't completely there. Not nearly as present as I am now. There was no way for me to know or realize that until I stopped. I didn't know there was another way. I didn't know what truly present really meant. I didn't know I had more to give.

I now know that whenever my kid walks through the door on a Saturday night at 11 pm, I am fully available and present to meet him and handle whatever may come my way. And if you're a parent of teenagers, there will be shit that comes your way. The feelings of integrity, pride, and peace that comes with being ready for that is priceless. More than that, *my kids* now know that there's no checking out for me. *They* know I'm available to them no matter the time of day or what's going on, and that gives them a sense of peace too. We want more than anything to provide safety and comfort to our kids, don't we? We long for that so much. There are so many forces in this world working against that, but we are in control of whether we are a source of security and solace for our kids. And yet, drinking robs us of the ability to truly do that.

I can't tell you the number of conversations I've had with my kids and their friends on Friday and Saturday nights that never would have happened when I was drinking. Most of these interactions are not deep, earth-shattering conversations. It's just BS'ing about whatever teens are talking about at the time. But it gives me a chance to listen. I listen to what interests them, to their opinions. I listen to how they react to things, how they talk about other people, and how they interact with each other. I also use it to observe. Who's happy, who's sad. Who's driving the conversation and who's hesitant to speak up. What's the dynamic like between the kids. You can pick up a lot about your own kid and others just by observing when they hang out with each other.

These moments—all these little moments that may seem inconsequential at the time—are so important to building connection, comfort, and trust with your kids—especially teens. What they say is true: the little things are the big things. These moments add up. They help with the bond between you and your kids. They foster trust. They help your kids (and their friends) feel comfortable talking to you. With teens especially, that's what you want more than anything. They're not going to tell you everything, but you want them to feel safe and comfortable coming to you with things that are bothering them. Being there at 11 pm on a Friday night—truly being there—goes a long way toward getting to that point.

159

Todd Kinney

Anyone with teenagers knows that they're hardly ever prepared or willing to discuss big life issues when you want to. You never know when that moment is going to come, but I can tell you from experience that it's never on your terms. It has to be on their terms. And you never know when that opportunity is going to present itself. If they walk into the kitchen at 10 pm on a weeknight and you notice that they're engaging with you, you stay there and see where it goes—even if you were just about to head into your room to go to bed. If you're having a good conversation with one of your teens, but the game that you've been looking forward to all day is on, you put the game on the back burner. If you're working and a kid comes into your office just to make small talk, the work can wait. If you're getting ready to start on that to-do list that needs to get completed this weekend, but your teen decides then is a good time for a chat, you worry about the list later.

When I was drinking, my window for those opportunities to present themselves was smaller. It was smaller because I was busy drinking during times when my kids might present themselves. But it also was smaller because drinking and everything that came with it took up so much space in my head. It intruded. If I wasn't actively drinking, I was thinking about it. If something took me away from drinking, I was annoyed and resentful. Whatever it was that took me away from my drinking didn't get my whole self. I blamed my annoyance on something else (usually my kids)—anything but the real cause. Who wants to admit that you're annoyed with your kid because he's taking you away from drinking? It's much easier just to say that you're annoyed with the kid himself, or the situation, or whatever.

My fourteen-year-old's friends in particular have taken an interest in my sobriety. They ask me really interesting, probing questions about why I quit and what I like about sobriety. It's fascinating to me that they're so interested in it. They're drawn to the subject. I love that they are. I'm not naive enough to think that none of them will drink because of me, but it's so affirming to me that they're curious about my decision to quit drinking. It's encouraging to me that they're thinking about something like that at their age. I sure wasn't and, as I've noted, I didn't even know it was an option. They've told me they're proud of me, which fills me up like few things do.

I've received the following text messages from them the past couple of years:

"Hey congrats on being sober for three years now. I'm looking forward to seeing your book. I always enjoy hearing your stories about you being sober and I find it so interesting because it's such a different point of view than we are used to hearing from our own parents."

"Hi Todd. Just wanted to say congrats on 3 years. You are an inspiration to many, and I can't wait to read your book."

"Congrats Todd on your third year of being sober!!!! I'm so proud of you, you inspire me so much just to be a better man. Congratulations!"

"HAPPY BIRTHDAY TODD!!! Thank you for all you do for me, I appreciate you so much. Seriously I don't know what I would do if I didn't have the best 2nd dad in the world, love you Todd!"

"Happy Father's Day Todd, I couldn't ask for a better 2nd dad, hope you have the best day ever!"

"Happy Father's Day Todd. I'm so thankful that I have such a kind human like you in my life, I appreciate you so much Todd!"

I doubt I would have cultivated the relationships I have with these boys that prompted these texts if I hadn't quit drinking. I also doubt that these boys truly appreciate and understand how much these texts mean to me now and always will.

Since I quit, I've observed how much our kids notice our (their parents') drinking. They notice it all. I've had kids tell me they wish their parents were sober. I've had kids tell me they think their parents drink too much. Had I not stopped drinking, my kids would have said these very same things to a sober dad. I used to wonder (although I never went into it too deeply), "Do my kids notice my drinking? Does it weigh on them? Do they wish I'd drink less? Does my drinking have a negative effect on them?" What I've discovered since I quit is that the answer to each of those questions is a resounding yes.

Landon came home one night and said that a friend had invited him to Lake Okoboji and he was trying to decide whether he wanted to go. He seemed unsure about it. I asked him if he was having reservations. He mentioned that the friend's dad liked to drink. He was concerned about being on a boat with him.

I told Landon that it was very mature for him to be thinking about that. "I get it from you, Dad." Some real-time feedback! For a split second, I felt like I was doing something right. Teenagers are tough. It's hard to get inside their heads. This was a small but meaningful glimpse inside Landon's head and an outward sign that my sobriety was having a positive impact on my kids. Of course, I would have talked to Landon about the dangers of drinking if I still drank, but how much credibility would I have had? Yes, I'm an adult drinking legally, so that's some distinction. But Landon had seen me drink in excess enough times that a lot of my words would have rung hollow for him. Let's face it, when your kids know that you abuse alcohol on a regular basis, you lose credibility when talking to them about the dangers of abusing alcohol. It's hard enough to reach our teenagers, we don't need to make it harder on ourselves.

What these stories taught me, and what I hope I'm conveying to you, is that there's a better way to live out there. Something that you're not even aware of at this moment or can't fully comprehend. I certainly couldn't before I quit drinking. If you had told me about it, I wouldn't have believed it. It would've sounded okay, but surely not as good as a life that included drinking beer. I'm here to tell you, it's way better. When, at four months sober, the lawyer from Orlando texted me, "At this point (over 4 years now), I can't imagine a circumstance that would cause me to go back," I didn't fully appreciate what he meant. I do now.

I'm also showing my kids that there's a different way. They see a *lot* of drinking. Drinking at meals, on vacations, at peoples' houses, at sporting events, when they're out of town for sports trips. You name it, there's alcohol there. We adults know that drinking is everywhere. Well, kids see it too. They're taught—whether we mean to do so or not—that it's just what you do. Drinking is what's normal, almost expected even. Drinking will accompany everything in life, and that's just the way it is. That's what I thought, based on how I grew up. I didn't know any different, I didn't know anything else was even an option.

My kids may decide on their own to drink, they may not. But regardless, I'm showing them that drinking doesn't have to be part of it all. I can live a (more) fulfilling life without it. And when I do it in an environment where almost everyone else is drinking (which is almost always the case), I'm also showing them the value of living with your integrity, even when it goes against the grain of what everyone else is doing. That is such a valuable example to show kids, especially teens and preteens.

The questions started that Saturday morning in the Chinese restaurant parking lot. I didn't dwell on them for long then. But as my kids got older, and as my drinking continued without meaningful change despite all my efforts, the questions returned. Again and again.

> Am I being the best dad I can be?
>
> Am I setting the best example for my kids?
>
> Am I proud of myself?
>
> Can I do better than this?
>
> Do I want to continue risking not being able to step up in a crisis if it hits at 11:00 on a Saturday night?
>
> Do my kids deserve better than this?
>
> Do I want to be the parent who is always chasing that buzz, or the one who is there for his kids?
>
> Do I want to be the parent who is distracted by and preoccupied with the next drink, or the one that my kid can bring something serious to at 10:00 on a Friday night?
>
> Do I want to be impaired or prepared?

For the longest time, I took the route that made me a worse parent. I chose alcohol over my kids, over my wife, over just about everything else. I wasn't conscious of what I was doing, but that doesn't make it any less true. Sure, I was still "there" for them. But too often I wasn't there for them. Not like a parent should be. Not like I am now. I was there for them—unless. Unless it was Friday at 10 pm and I wasn't safe to drive. Unless there was a happy hour I wanted to go to. Unless I had been golfing earlier and had too many beers. Unless we had people over and were drinking with them. Unless I was hung over from the night before. Unless alcohol, the always-reliable, ever-present Great Intruder, was involved. They say love is spelled T-I-M-E. There is no greater thief of time than alcohol.

There are only so many things we can control when it comes to our kids. Parenthood sometimes feels like you've been pushed down a hill on a sled and you have no idea how to stop it or even slow it down. Knowing that I'm so much more available to my kids and feel so much more capable of handling whatever life is going to throw my way makes that ride down-hill feel not quite as scary. We have one shot at this parenting thing. Don't we want to do everything possible to ensure "success" (whatever that may look like)? Of course we do. We're sold a lie that alcohol makes parenting easier, that we need and deserve that drink at the end of a long day to deal with the stress of having kids. For years, I bought into that lie. I embraced it. But now, having parented both as a drinker and as a sober dad, I can tell you unequivocally that drinking makes parenting harder, not easier. I am a better dad sober.

***

Lest you think that all these stories represent shining beacons of hope that put tears in my eyes, let me tell you about the day I decided to sit down and talk to my oldest kid about my issues with alcohol, how much I enjoyed life without it, and everything I'd learned from quitting. Austin is very similar to me. He has a similar personality and has issues with impulse control and decision-making. He also has obsessive behaviors. He reminds me a lot of myself at his age. I'm almost certain he's going to drink in a similar manner as I did. That worries me. I know I can't make him not drink. And I know that me repeating over and over "you shouldn't drink" will have zero impact and probably push him closer to drinking. What I can do is live my life of sobriety as an example for him and impart knowl-edge when I think he'll be receptive to it. And so, one summer day when I had about twenty months of sobriety under my belt, I decided it was the right time to deliver a speech that I was certain would impact him for a long time.

I rehearsed the speech in my head over and over. I mulled the main points I wanted to get across to him. I thought about the best way to deliver it. It was going to be nonpreachy and nonjudgmental. It was going to be something that resonated with a fifteen-year-old. He would be so moved by my words that he would tell his friends about it. Most of all, it would be something he would remember for the rest of his life.

I sat down with him and launched into my speech. He put his phone down. He was looking me in the eye. He was absorbing it. He was listening to me—*really* listening, not just half-ass teenager listening. I went down the list of my main points, in a conversational tone, so he would be more apt to take it all in and process it. I was making my points, but not overdoing it. It seemed to be working. I was very proud of how it was going. I was patting myself on the back for being such a great dad. I was sure he'd have some questions or some sort of encouraging response.

When I was done, I asked, "What do you think?"

He responded, "Do you know what time the Apple store opens today?"

CHAPTER TWENTY

Be (ing) a Man!

"Alcohol is necessary for a man so that he can have a good opinion of himself, undisturbed by the facts." [8]

When I quit drinking, I read a lot of "quit lit." I devoured anything I could get my hands on. I took nuggets of wisdom from everything I read. Just reading someone else's story fueled me to keep going. It gave me hope, it inspired me. It made me want to do what they had done already. And it made me feel like it all was possible. With the exception of *Dry* by Augusten Burroughs, everything I read was written by a woman. TLC—the online sobriety-support group started by Laura McKowen, and the most welcoming community I've ever been a part of—was at least 90% female. There were countless women's support groups on line, but very few geared toward men. There were a couple of sobriety podcasts that featured male and female cohosts, but that landscape also was dominated by females. Everywhere I turned to for sobriety support was female-centered.

There is nothing inherently wrong with that, of course. At first, I felt more comfortable interacting with women when it came to sobriety. It felt safer. I didn't have to worry about being ostracized and made fun of by a fellow dude. But I did find myself sometimes wishing that I knew more guys that I could talk to about sobriety. Whenever I saw another guy in one of the TLC Zoom meetings, I would perk up, like the new kid at school who sees someone who might become his friend. "I wonder if we would get along," I'd think to myself.

It's not lost on me that women and minorities find themselves in these types of situations almost every day. Many have walked into a boardroom or similar setting and been confronted with a room full of white males—and those settings are not always as welcoming as TLC. As a white male who has benefited from nearly every possible built-in advantage one could ask for, I felt silly and unworthy for complaining about struggling to find people who "looked like me" and were going through the same thing. But addiction and alcohol abuse don't discriminate. It hits white males just like it hits females, minorities, and everyone else. And we all need to see examples of people we identify with the most going through the same thing and living to tell about it. That's why the story from the lawyer in Orlando, who looked very much like me, was so powerful.

While females face their own unique issues when it comes to alcohol abuse (the "mommy wine" culture is real), males do too. There's a unique pressure to drink if you're a male. It's expected, and there's a feeling of "less than" if you don't. There are a few qualities that society has dictated that you must possess to be a "proper" male. Near the top of that list is that you must be a drinker, someone who enjoys beers with other males who similarly enjoy beer. Beers with the guys—what's more masculine than that?

For the majority of my life, I not only bought into this narrative, I embraced it. That's what successful, fun, cool guys did—we drank together. Drinking together was where connections happened, where relationships flourished, where memories were made. That's where life was lived! I was someone who was always up for a drink because that's what cool guys did. That made me a good friend and the "right" kind of male. It was part of the fabric of who I was. "Let's go get a drink" was an instant connector and bond builder, whether I'd known the person for 20 minutes or 20 years.

Guys who didn't drink? They were kind of weird and not to be trusted fully. They certainly weren't people that I would choose to spend time with. How boring would that be? Take drinking away from a man's life, and it's like you're cutting off a limb.

Todd Kinney

Laura McKowen says:

> "When people get sober, they don't only give up alcohol, they give up an entire identity." [9]

That's exactly how it felt for me. No wonder it took me six years of evaluating my drinking before I decided to quit.

Every activity involving friends or socializing—golf, travel, tailgating, hanging out watching sports—for me, the *drinking* was the activity. It wasn't the event, the conversation, or the game. It was the drinking that accompanied those things. That's what made it magical—having the beers. The golf or whatever wasn't enough by itself. The comradery itself wasn't enough. The social interaction itself wasn't enough. All those things were fun, sure, but not fun enough to stand on their own. But throw drinking into the mix? Now that's something different. That's something worth doing. In my mind, it was the drinking that made it quality time with friends. How sad is that?

Drinking developed into this almost mythological idea to me. There was this whole "thing" around drinking that became so central to my idea of what was fun, what constituted "quality time," and what was necessary for something to be worthwhile. I think it was a combination of how much I liked to drink and the powerful effects of alcohol marketing.

The alcohol industry is a billion-dollar marketing machine. Billion-dollar marketing machines work extremely well. Quitting meant ripping a huge chunk of my identity away. It felt like I would have to become a completely different person. [Side note: It actually does involve becoming a different person! But in a really, really good way. At the time, though, it feels like it's in a really bad way.] It felt that way because I so closely associated drinking with positive things. It meant I was fun, outgoing, up for a good time, a "guy's guy" that you can have a drink with. That's who I wanted to be to my friends, that's how I wanted people to think of me. Never mind all the horrible things about drinking—I left those out of my drinking identity. Refer back to: billion-dollar marketing machines are very effective. I simply omitted the hangovers, the shame and embarrassment, the regret, the blackouts. I knew they were there, of course. But when I was building the identity of Todd the drinker in my head, that meant only the "good" parts of drinking. If I took that away and became Todd, the guy who doesn't drink, what kind of man would I be?

I was scared of who I would be as a nondrinker. Scared that people wouldn't like me. Scared that people would make fun of me. Scared that I'd be left out. Scared that life would pass me by.

On top of that, it's not breaking news that guys have a harder time talking about their emotions than women do. We certainly struggle with being vulnerable. And deciding to quit drinking makes you vulnerable, if nothing else. Actually, I've never struggled much with talking about my emotions. When we were growing up, my parents fostered a very open atmosphere where talking about things was encouraged. I'm very thankful for that. But guys in general have long been taught not to talk openly about our feelings. To not be vulnerable. We have to be tough and strong and show no weakness. We're supposed to be the protector of our families. And if we're in charge of protecting our family, how can we ever show any weakness? If we do, we're failing in the most central job we have. If we can't protect our family, what are we even good for?

All this is changing, of course, and that's a good thing. But these messages have been pounded into men and women for generations. They don't go away overnight. And the bridge between understanding that its okay (even healthy) to talk about your feelings, fears, and vulnerability, and actually doing it, can be a long one. Even for someone like me who doesn't have a lot of trouble talking about my emotions, it was difficult and scary for me to express what I was feeling about my alcohol use. I certainly couldn't do it with any of my drinking friends. It wasn't until I found the community of TLC that I truly started talking with others about my alcohol issues outside of my therapist's office, and that was mostly with women. It's so important for us guys to tell the truth about what's really going on inside. I always make a point to tell my kids when I'm going to see my therapist. I want to normalize it for them and let them know that talking about things with a mental health professional is healthy.

Whenever I found myself in a social setting with other guys, my anxiety over not drinking would spike. I felt like an outcast that much more. Like I needed some sort of excuse besides just not wanting to drink—you know, a "legitimate" one. All the regular awkwardness of not drinking and early sobriety was more pronounced when I was in a setting full of guys than when I was with females or even in mixed company. I was not as self-conscious about it when I was around women. They were less judgmental. I felt they would "get it" more. I was much less concerned about getting shit from women than I was from my male friends. I think women are quicker to acknowledge and appreciate the self-reflection involved with quitting drinking than most guys are.

Hell, all these things are the very reasons that a lot of men have drinking issues in the first place. We have fears and feelings that we don't want to express or don't know how to express. So we "drink at them," to cope. We drink to numb them. Drinking becomes the only way we "deal" with them at all. The feelings don't go away, of course. Drinking at them never solves anything. It just leads to a cycle of more drinking, less dealing with the feelings, then more shitty feelings about the drinking, which make us feel worse than we did in the first place. Rinse and repeat. It's a terrible cycle, like a petri dish for shame and self-loathing. When it comes down to it, the root cause of so many drinking issues is the inability to process and address feelings and emotions in a healthy way. The one thing guys universally have struggled with over time is processing, expressing, and addressing our feelings and emotions. We've been taught not to do that for generations. It's no wonder that we guys struggle with drinking and find it difficult to start down the path of quitting.

If you're a guy out there who feels like drinking is tied too closely to your identity to give it up, or that you'll be perceived as weak if you admit you have alcohol issues, or that you'll lose some of your "manliness" if you quit, I thought all of that too. And I was wrong about it all. I'm here to tell you you're not alone. There are thousands of us out there. I can't tell you how helpful it was for me to sit down and talk to other guys about this stuff. It validated everything for me. It made me feel like I wasn't defective. It made me feel like it was going to be okay. Find someone, anyone, to reach out to. Reach out to me. Just know that there are others out there who feel the same way you do. Some have found some of the answers, and others are still looking. But they're out there. And they're a lot like you.

Ironically, a big reason why I feel lighter and calmer in sobriety is that I just feel more authentic. I feel more like me. It took me a while before I identified that feeling. The idea of feeling *more* authentic after removing alcohol from my life seemed backward and impossible. Alcohol was such a big part of my identity, I thought I would feel *less* like myself after I quit drinking (and sometimes I did). It didn't make sense at the time that taking alcohol away would make me feel like I was living more as my true self. But I was, and it felt mysteriously, surprisingly good. *Really* good, and a different kind of good. It was yet another truth that sobriety revealed that I couldn't run from. But I didn't want to.

There's an episode of *Your Honor* where Bryan Cranston's character says:

> "There is a world of difference between who we are and who we want to be." [10]

Removing alcohol from my life made that gap smaller for me. I feel so much more in line with the person I want to be. The person I'm meant to be. The best version of me. I am a better father, husband, and person as a nondrinker, and I like myself more. What's more masculine than that?

CHAPTER TWENTY-ONE

None of the Bad Things Happened

The biggest thing, by far, that kept me from giving up alcohol was fear. When you think of how ingrained alcohol is in our lives—work, social events, at home, everywhere we go—it's no surprise that the idea of giving it up is scary. It's not like giving up pizza. The mere suggestion by my therapist back in 2013 that I take a three-month break made me anxious and panicked—and I was already at the place where I knew I needed to do *something*.

I couldn't fathom how I was supposed to do all of life's events over those next three months without alcohol. Trips. Tailgating. Parties. Thanksgiving! Christmas! New Year's Eve—who does New Year's sober?! Work events. And those were only the big events, it didn't even count the random Friday night happy hours or the lunches and dinners at sports bars with our kids' teams and parents. How in the world was I supposed to do this? It was like trying to figure out how to do life without being able to see or hear. That's how overwhelming and scary it was for me.

The crippling sense of fear associated with the idea of giving up alcohol that so many of us have is a testament to the marketing prowess of the booze industry. For me, the fear was powerful enough that it stopped any contemplation of quitting in its tracks for a long time. It was just too much, so it was easier to not go there. It was indicative of how much I relied on alcohol just to do life. If you had asked me at the time whether I relied or was dependent on it, I would have said no (while bristling at the question on the inside). After all, I didn't drink during the week. How can someone "rely" on something if he can go Monday through Thursday without it? However, looking back to 2013, when I did my first three-month break, it should have set off more alarm bells that the thought of giving it up completely was so debilitating.

If the thought of giving up alcohol scares you, as it did me, ask yourself why. What scares you about it? Don't stop at the first thing that comes to mind. My first thought was always something that, while true, was superficial. Something along the lines of, "How boring! Who wants to do sporting events and holidays without alcohol? That's lame." But there was more to it than that, if I was honest with myself. I didn't know who I would be without alcohol. Drinking was so central to everything I did that it didn't feel like I was just giving up drinking, it felt like I was giving up life.

So ask yourself, what *really* scares you about it? Dig beyond your surface-level stuff. You don't think you can do it? You don't think you'd want to live a life without alcohol? People will think you're weird? People will think you must have had a really bad problem? You won't be any fun? You won't be able to get through a day without that drink waiting at the end? Whatever you're thinking, I can promise you I thought it too.

I had a whole list of horrible things that I was 100% convinced would happen to me if I gave up alcohol. Guess what? None of them happened. I was wrong about it all. Here are some of the things I was afraid of:

- People wouldn't want to hang out with me.

o <u>What I thought then:</u> I don't really want to hang out with nondrinkers, so why would anyone want to hang out with me if I quit?

o <u>What I know now:</u> Full disclosure: There will be people you stop hanging out with (or hang out with less) if you stop drinking. Another full disclosure: You won't care. There are a couple of people in my life who I discovered I was connected to mainly by alcohol. Take that away and I didn't really enjoy hanging out with them very much. They may feel the same about me. That's okay. Aside from those people, I'm happy to report that I haven't been excommunicated from my social circle. My interests certainly have shifted, and I don't want to do some of the things I wanted to do before. Turns out, much of what I wanted to do before socially revolved around my ability to drink. I would tolerate so many social situations simply because they allowed me to drink, and I just don't have much interest in those things anymore. If you need alcohol to enjoy certain people or activities, you probably need to find new people to hang out with and new things to do.

Your true friends are your true friends. That will remain the case even when you stop drinking. I'm fortunate to have some rock-solid friendships in my life. People I've known for decades, some literally my whole life. Those relationships didn't go anywhere when I stopped drinking. In fact, they're better now.

- People would think I was a raging alcoholic and would judge me simplistically as "a bad person."

o <u>What I thought then</u>: If you have to quit drinking, you must have a real problem. As in, a vodka-for-breakfast-type problem. A losing-jobs-type problem. A cops-involved-type problem. Quitting is for people who failed, who couldn't get their shit together, and who were hanging on in their lives by a thread.

o <u>What I know now</u>: Honestly, I don't know what most people think about what my drinking was like. I'm sure there are some who think it was much different than it actually was. Here is what I do know: I had so many people reach out to me after I "came out" on social media on my one-year anniversary of quitting. So many who struggled with similar issues or who knew someone close to them who did. I had people come to me and ask for help—I still do. I had people say they quit for the same reasons I did—only they made up reasons for quitting because they weren't sure what people would think if they spoke their truth. I had many, many people thank me for telling my story. The feedback I got was so positive and so heart-warming. People don't judge you like you think they will—not anyone who matters, anyway.

Think about it this way: Would you judge someone who gave up drinking to make a positive change in his life? I know I wouldn't. So I don't know why I thought others would judge me. But that's what we humans do, that's how our brains work. What's great about where I'm at now is that I don't care what people think my drinking was like. It doesn't matter. What matters is that my alcohol use—or whatever you want to label or call it—was causing problems in my life, and I wanted to make a change. So I did.

At the time I quit, I was examining all this through an outside lens. I was looking at it from the point of "what are others going to think?" This is a fairly standard reaction, I think. But it's also foolish. One, because we're usually wrong about what people are going to think. We focus on the worst part of it. Say, for example, that you're thinking about doing something that 99 people will view positively and one person will view negatively. What do we focus on? That one person, of course. Does that make any sense?

The second reason it's foolish to examine things through an outside lens is that that's not the lens that matters. Your lens is what matters. It sounds so simple when I write it down and read it on paper. But we all fall into the trap of becoming way more concerned with what other people think rather than focusing on what's best for us. We let others' opinions—or our perceptions of others' opinions—drive too much of our behavior. As I sit here today (four years sober, at the time of this writing), I can tell you that for me the benefits of a sober life so far outweigh a life with alcohol that the concern about what others think has vanished.

Matthew McConaughey—who I'm convinced would want to be best friends if we ever met in person—writes in his book *Greenlights* about "voluntary obligations." He calls them the "You versus You obligations." They're the things we know in our gut to be true that guide us, or should anyway, if we're living right. Secrets "in the court of our own conscience." [11]

I wish I had understood this concept more when I was deciding whether to quit and when I was early on in sobriety. If I had, I wouldn't have wasted so much time and energy worrying about what other people were going to think. Nobody else has to understand your decision to give up alcohol. And it's not your job to make them understand. One second spent worrying about what someone thinks about your decision to change your drinking habits is one second too many. When you're following your gut and living in alignment with your voluntary obligations, you can never go wrong.

- You need to hit rock bottom—spectacularly—before you quit.

  o <u>What I thought then</u>: Rock bottom is waking up in a ditch. It's your third DUI. It's landing in the back of a cop car. It's losing a job because you were drinking too much. None of that has happened to me, so I don't have a rock bottom. Without a "sufficient" rock bottom, I don't need to quit.

  o <u>What I know now:</u> What I did have was a hundred smaller, less-spectacular rock bottoms. Moments that, standing alone, *could* have served as THE rock bottom, but didn't. Some of them certainly should have. Looking back, on the one hand I'm surprised that some of them by themselves didn't jolt me into getting sober. But on the other hand, given what I know now about the rationalizing and negotiating I did with my drinking, I'm not that surprised. And in the end, that's not really important. What's important is that the "little" rock bottoms eventually piled high enough that they tipped the scale for me.

It doesn't matter what your rock bottom is. You don't even have to have one. We need to get rid of this idea that we HAVE to hit some sort of rock bottom to do something about our alcohol use. Rock bottom doesn't have to be a singular place or event. Rock bottom can be a gradual slide—it often is. Or it can be several "minor" rock bottoms. It can be waking up the next morning not remembering going to bed. It can be driving drunk and getting away with it. It can be not remembering conversations from the night before. It can be checking your phone with that sense of dread about what you may have texted or posted the night before. It can be waking up in your own house not sure whether your kids are there or they slept at a friend's house. It can be your son bringing up a conversation that you don't remember. It can be jumping in a pool with your clothes on at a work event. It can be a DUI. It can be acting in a way you're not proud of. It can be walking around downtown after a high school reunion with a dead phone and not being able to find an Uber. Or it can be as simple as not liking how drinking makes you feel. It can be feeling sick of your own bullshit. It can be wanting to improve your relationship with your kids or your partner. It can be simply wanting to improve your health. It can be *anything*.

Yet the idea of quitting on my own, without some traumatic event to justify it, was completely foreign to me. For so long, all my thoughts about quitting were tied to something happening that would force me to quit—where I simply would have no choice. It got to the point where a small part of me was subconsciously hoping for something bad to happen just so it would prompt me to quit.

For years, my internal debate centered around this question: Is my drinking bad enough that I should make a change? I was looking at it the wrong way. The better question to ask is: Is this good enough for me to continue down this road? Is there a better way? And when you're wondering whether the life you're living is good enough, ask yourself this: How do I know whether it is? How do you truly know? You don't until you've genuinely tried another path. Give that other road a try. See whether you like it. If you don't, you can get back on the road you were on. Drinking isn't going anywhere, you can always go back. At least you tried and now you know. But give it a try—a real try. That means time. That means not bailing on the new road the first, second, or third time that things get tough and uncomfortable.

- I wouldn't make any more memories.

o <u>What I thought then:</u> All my memories—the stories my friends and I tell over and over and over again, laughing just as hard each time—involve alcohol. How in the world can I ever make new memories if I remove alcohol from the equation? It's impossible. It's hard to make memories sitting at home staring out your window, which is what sober people do, right?

- <u>What I know now</u>: I have a folder on my phone called "sober thankful." Whenever I have a moment when I'm feeling particularly grateful to be sober, I take my phone out, document it with a photo, and put it in that folder. As of this moment, there are 254 pictures in it—each one a memory I thought I would never make. Each one represents a memory that fills me with a sense of gratitude and happiness different from, and better than, what my drinking memories ever did.

It's a picture of Scarlett and two of her friends golfing, because I happily took them instead of staying back with other adults who were drinking. Rather than be annoyed that the activity was interrupting my drinking, I felt grateful that I got to watch these three girls do something fun on a perfect summer night.

It's a screen shot of a post a friend made thanking me for helping her reach her one-year sober anniversary.

It's a picture of a sunrise at Lake Tahoe whose breathtaking beauty I never would have discovered during my drinking days.

It's a picture of my son on a random Friday night at 10 pm to document the conversation we'd just had that never would have occurred if I'd been drinking.

It's a picture of my kids and their friends enjoying themselves in the pool on a Saturday night because I was sitting back just soaking it all in and feeling grateful that I was present in that moment instead of wondering what my next drink should be or whether I needed to slow down.

It's a picture of a cup of decaf coffee and a book I sat with in a hotel lobby in Washington, DC, while traveling for work, because I liked doing that so much more than sitting in a bar drinking too much, as I'd often done previously while traveling by myself.

It's a picture of my daughter at a board-game café, where we went between her basketball games one weekend. We had so much fun there, playing checkers and drinking hot chocolate. It was infinitely better than sitting in a sports bar, me focused on how many beers I could have between games and her on her phone.

It's a random picture of nature, which brings me joy that I never knew before.

It's a picture of me on the golf course with Austin, knowing that I was present for the whole experience instead of focusing on drinking.

It's a picture of the kids on Christmas morning, knowing that I was clearheaded and not beating myself up for drinking too much the night before.

It's a screen shot of a text from a friend, telling me I'm an inspiration to him.

It's a picture of Landon and me at a football game, knowing that the game wasn't affected by the Great Intruder and loving sober game days so much more than drinking ones.

It's a picture of Bryant Park in New York City, where I was when I realized, after my text exchange with my therapist, that I was liking myself more sober.

It's a picture of me playing four-square in the street with Scarlett and her friends at 10:00 on a Friday night, which I enjoyed so much more than my usual drinking Friday nights.

These are pictures of life happening. Each one represents a moment that filled me with a sense of gratitude, purpose, and joy that even the best drinking nights couldn't compete with.

- I would never have fun again because sobriety would be so boooooooring.

o <u>What I thought then</u>: Drinking = fun. Fun = drinking. That's life's equation. Is it even possible to have fun—I mean, real fun—without drinking? I don't think so. Every instance of fun I can think of involved drinking. How in the world can people have fun without alcohol being involved? It's like trying to get full without eating food.

The first word that always comes to mind when I hear about someone who doesn't drink is boring. Their life had to be boring, there was no other way around it. How could it not be?

o <u>What I know now:</u> You know how you look back on things we used to do and you can't believe it was socially acceptable: riding in cars without seatbelts, smoking in airplanes, spanking our kids? I don't mean looking back with judgment, just with disbelief that nobody knew any better. That's the same way I feel about thinking that I'd never have fun again without alcohol.

For one, as I get further away from my drinking life, I realize that drinking was not as much fun as I thought it was. Sure, it had its moments. But when I step back and objectively look at drinking through a sober lens, it's not everything I thought it was. There's the initial "ahhhh" feeling with that first drink. Then there's the initial buzz that feels good. After that, though . . . what exactly are we buying with alcohol?

- We get more numb
- We start to forget things
- Our ability to make rational decisions diminishes
- We repeat ourselves
- We get louder
- We get sloppier
- The chances of putting ourselves in dangerous situations goes up
- The chances of us saying or doing something we'll regret go up
- The chances of feeling like shit the next day go way up.

The list goes on and on. Does any of that sound like fun? If we were talking about anything other than alcohol, would you ever think of engaging in an activity that had those side effects? If we're really honest about what alcohol does to us, it doesn't seem like nearly as much fun.

But more than that, I've discovered that everything I do is more fun sober:

- Going to the gym clearheaded and not sluggish from the night before kicks the endorphin high up a notch.

- Hanging out with my kids, or my wife, or really doing anything in life without the intrusion of "when can I have that first drink" or "I could be drinking now" allows me to be present in a way I never was before. The Great Intruder is gone. Everything is more fulfilling when you're present. Who knew?

• Going on vacation and being free of the regret and shame-filled mornings feels phenomenal. So does not needing three days to recover once you get home.

• Work events without the effort of staying in control are actually more enjoyable. (I haven't jumped into any pools with my clothes on since getting sober!)

• Handling the stresses of everyday life, big and little, is infinitely easier with the calmness and peace of mind I have when sober, which I never knew when I was drinking.

This didn't happen overnight. There were social and family events early on when it felt more like I was just getting through them than truly enjoying them. But that's part of the process. The first football game, the first vacation, the first party—those can be tough. But they get easier, little by little. If you're going to get to the place where you enjoy all those things more when sober, you have to get through the first one.

In *We Are the Luckiest*, Laura McKowen writes about the "nice little life" that a friend, Sara, had discovered in sobriety. Laura, who was early in her sobriety when she heard her friend describe her new life, initially was underwhelmed because it felt like the opposite of the "big, vast, expansive, exciting" life that she longed for. But eventually she came to view her friend's description in a much different light:

> "How wrong I had been in my understanding of Sara's words. How wrong I had been in my understanding of nearly everything that makes this life worth living. I understood her expression "a nice little life" to mean a paltry, pale existence. I didn't know the difference between the cheap, thin drama of a drinking life and the rich, layered texture of a sober one. Which is to say an *awake* one. I mistook the limited expression of outer life for the unlimited expanse of the inner one. I didn't see—couldn't possibly have seen—all that would come forth from simply allowing space to exist." [12]

Todd Kinney

I had a very similar initial reaction to the idea of "a nice little life" as Laura did. Even reading about how wrong she realized she'd been didn't sway me completely. Like Laura, at that stage of my sobriety I couldn't possibly comprehend the beauty and magic of what "a nice little life" meant.

I do now. A "nice little life" is fuller than my old life. It's calmer. It's more peaceful. It's better. It's happier. It's easier. It's the opposite of what I thought it was when I first heard of it. My nice little life has gifted me a sense of peace and calmness that I never had before as an adult. If that's boring, I'll sign up for it every time.

The best testimony I can give is this: I've done all these life events both as a drinker and a nondrinker—and it's no contest which is more fun.

Being totally and completely convinced that all these bad things were going to happen, and then having none of them happen, opened my mind like few things in my life have. It's removed so much of the stigma and anxiety around BIG changes. Change isn't as scary now—how can it be? I made a decision to give up something that I thought I couldn't live without, and I ended up discovering a life that I didn't know existed. The downsides weren't downsides, and the upsides were greater than I possibly could have fathomed. This doesn't guarantee that every change I make from here on out will be as profound (or even work out), but it does mean that a lot of the angst, stress, and natural pushback that accompanies the idea of big changes has melted away. That, in and of itself, is a powerful life lesson.

CHAPTER TWENTY-TWO

It's Right in Front of You

"When it feels scary to jump, that's exactly WHEN you jump. Otherwise you end up staying in the same place your whole life. And that I can't do." [13]

Whatever your motivation is for reading this book, I salute you. Not for reading the book (although I thank you for that!). I applaud you for having the courage to evaluate your life, for evaluating something in your life in the name of improving yourself. That's a good thing. Please don't lose sight of that. Believe it or not, not a lot of people have the courage to do that, especially when it comes to alcohol. You do. Whether you're on Day 1 or Day 500, whether you're desperate to give up alcohol or you're just dipping your toe in the water, it takes courage to do what you're doing.

Drinking is terribly unhealthy for us. The adverse health consequences are well-known. Alcohol is the unhealthiest substance most of us put in our bodies on a regular basis. It's classified as a Group 1 carcinogen—the highest-risk group, the same one that contains asbestos, radioactive materials, and tobacco.[14] It increases your risk for at least eight types of cancer. [15] Even one drink a day can increase your risk for certain types of cancer, including breast cancer.[16] It's the leading modifiable risk factor for cancer in the United States.[17] In addition to cancer,

183

drinking increases your risk of chronic diseases such as high blood pressure, heart disease, stroke, liver disease, digestive problems, dementia, depression, and anxiety.[18] Alcohol interferes with the brain's ability to perform its most important functions.[19] In 2023, the World Health Organization issued a statement to the effect that there is no amount of alcohol consumption that is "safe," that doesn't affect your health.[20] From 2015 to 2019, alcohol killed more people than opiates,[21] and alcohol-related deaths only have increased since then.[22] Everyone knows that we have an "opioid crisis" in this country. Have you ever heard anyone say we have an "alcohol crisis"?

I don't say this to convince you to stop drinking because it's not good for you. I've always prioritized exercise and eating well, yet knowing that drinking was bad for me had zero impact on my drinking habits. Instead, I say this to highlight the grip that alcohol has on us individually and collectively as a society. Take smoking. Smoking is also very bad for your health. We know this and we accept it. But if you're a smoker and decide to quit, do you ever have to worry about being shunned by your friends? Do you worry about not being invited to social events anymore? Do you worry about how to explain your decision to quit smoking to all the people who'll ask and not understand? Do you worry about not having fun ever again if you quit smoking? Of course not.

Substitute anything for quitting smoking. Cutting sugar out of your diet. Starting to exercise. Eliminating soda. None of those questions enter the equation with those choices. But with drinking, all those things—and many more!—are part of the process. In our society, there is so much wrapped up in the decision to quit drinking. So much fear. So much trepidation. So much bullshit. So much baggage that's unique to quitting drinking. The stigma, the questions, the weird looks, the need to justify your decision, the fact that sometimes we have to physically avoid going to certain places because drinking is so prevalent. Alcohol is so ingrained in our daily lives, in our social lives, and in our society that quitting feels so heavy. It feels so hard. It can feel damn near impossible.

Yet at the end of the day, quitting drinking should be no different than any other decision you make to improve your life. It's no different than starting to exercise, quitting smoking, or eating better. You're choosing something healthier and leaving something unhealthy behind. There shouldn't be anything "controversial" about that. Nobody should feel the need to justify that kind of decision.

What if we changed the narrative? Instead of thinking of it as "I'm giving up alcohol," what if we thought of it as "I'm doing something that will…"

- Reduce my anxiety
- Make me a better parent
- Make me a better spouse
- Make me happier
- Make me feel better about myself
- Make me healthier in general
- Reduce my risk of cancer, heart disease, and other life-threatening ailments
- Make life easier and calmer
- Help me be more present

Would anyone argue with deciding to do something that offered all those benefits? Of course not. That's what you're doing when you decide to quit drinking.

If you're thinking about giving up alcohol, let me make a suggestion—one that I wish someone had made to me: trust your gut. Stop dismissing what it's telling you. Don't rely on other people for your truth. Don't borrow what you need from them to form what you want to be your truth. "You don't have a problem." "Sure, you like to drink, but look at so and so—he/she is much worse." "You just like to have fun, there's nothing wrong with that." I latched on to comments and thoughts like that for a long time to avoid my truth. Stop running from your inner voice. I ran from mine for too long.

If, at any point during my drinking days, I could have transported myself to now, where I know how much richer a sober life is than a drinking one, I would have quit on the spot. It would have been the easiest decision I'd ever made instead of one of the hardest. But that's not how life works.

You can't know these things until you do them. Until you experience them. Until you weather your own storm. You can't truly know what's on the other side until you get there. That's why they're hard decisions.

But you can take something from my story. You can take something from others' stories. That's what I did. You can let those stories make your leap a little less scary. They can be a crack of light in the darkness that you may feel you're walking into. They can be a glimmer of hope amid the uncertainty and fear. For a while, I thought all those people who talked about how magical sobriety was were all in on the same lie. Like it was one big, practical joke they had decided to play on the rest of the world. But I heard it enough that I couldn't help but wonder if there was something to it. And what I discovered was that not only is it not a lie, it's better than I ever imagined. It can be for you too.

About the Author

Todd Kinney is an attorney who lives in Omaha, Nebraska with his wife, four kids, and two wiener dogs. In his free time, he enjoys traveling, golf, hanging out with his family (when they let him), and spending an unhealthy amount of time and money supporting the Iowa Hawkeyes. He quit drinking in 2019 and considers it the best thing he's ever done for himself and his family.

How to contact Todd:
Tkinney111@gmail.com
Instagram: @tkinney111
Facebook
ToddKinney.com

Acknowledgements

Deanna. This book wouldn't have been written without you. In 2013, you set me down the path that led to where I am today. You did it with such grace, compassion, and wisdom that even I couldn't screw it up! I am forever grateful our paths crossed and hope you know how much of a role you played in the best decision I've ever made.

Chad, Tim, Gray, Ryan, Jay, Todd, Broc and Dan. You've been nothing but 100% supportive of my sobriety, something that did not surprise me in the least. One of my greatest blessings is my friendship with each one of you. I am lucky. I love you.

Cooper, Mack, Jack, John, Beckett, Max, and Madden. I hope you realize someday what your interest in my sobriety and in this book means to me. You are all wonderful young men with bright futures. I love you dudes.

Kerry, Mike, and Ann. Thank you for the use of your wonderful mountain home so I could (finally) finish this thing.

Angela. You lit the fire in me to kick this book into gear and finish it. You also provided countless hours of helpful feedback, encouragement and advice. I hope you know how much I value your input and what a big part of this book you were.

Peggi. If anyone was keeping track of the number of questions I asked you throughout this process, I think it's in the thousands! You were there every time I needed something and were constantly connecting me with someone helpful. I cherish our friendship and am grateful sobriety has connected us.

The Sullivans. When I was still antsy about what my future looked like as a non-drinker, I came to Colorado with Eli to visit you all. I didn't realize it at the time, but I was looking for a sign that something in my new life would feel the same as it did in my drinking life. Mission accomplished. I love you all like my own family.

Mom and Dad. If I thought you had been looking over at me in Arizona with contempt and shame, it may not have kickstarted this whole thing. But you would never do that, because that's not who you are. You are the best. I consider myself blessed beyond measure, and chief among my blessings is having parents who loved me unconditionally and instilled in me the intuition that led me down this path. I love you. And Dad, thank you for quitting and inspiring me to do the same.

Beth. Thank you for hanging in there with me. I wouldn't want to do this adventure with anyone else. I'm proud of us, and I love you. Thank you for telling me my parents were staring at me.

Austin, Landon, Eli, and Scarlett. They say you have to get sober for yourself, and that's true. I'll never know if I would have done it if you weren't in my life. But it doesn't matter. You are in my life, and I did do it, at least in the beginning, largely because of you. You made me want to be better. I will always be grateful for that. I love each of you beyond words.

Endnotes

1   Porter, William, *Alcohol Explained*, Monee, IL 2022.
2   Ibid
3   McKowen, Laura. *Push Off from Here: Nine Essential Truths to Get You Through Sobriety (and Everything Else)*, Ballantine Books 2023.
4   McKowen, Laura. *We Are the Luckiest: The Surprising Magic of a Sober Life,* New World Library, 2020.
5   Ibid
6   Brolin, Josh, in an Instagram post from November 1, 2021.
7   Ibid
8   Dune, Finlley Peter
9   McKowen, Laura, *Push Off from Here: Nine Essential Truths to Get You Through Sobriety (and Everything Else)*,Ballantine Books 2023.
10   "Part Nineteen", *Your Honor*, created by Peter Moffat, season 2, episode 9, CBS Television Studios, 2020.
11   Matthew McConaughey, *Greenlights,* Crown, *2020.*
12   McKowen, Laura, *We Are the Luckiest: The Surprising Magic of a Sober Life,* New World Library, 2020.
13   Chandor, J.C., (Director), 2014, *A Most Violent Year,*[Film], Washington Square Films.
14   https://www.who.int/europe/news/item/04-01-2023-no-level-of-alcohol-consumption-is-safe-for-our-health
15   https://www.cdc.gov/cancer/alcohol/reducing-excessive-alcohol-use/index.htm
16   Ibid
17   https://www.aacr.org/about-the-aacr/newsroom/news-releases/few-americans-are-aware-of-links-between-alcohol-and-cancer-risk/
18   https://www.cdc.gov/alcohol/fact-sheets/alcohol-use.htm
19   https://www.niaaa.nih.gov/publications/alcohol-and-brain-overview
20   https://www.who.int/europe/news/item/04-01-2023-no-level-of-alcohol-consumption-is-safe-for-our-health
21   https://www.caron.org/blog/alcohol-is-killing-more-people-than-fentanyl
22   Ibid

www.ingramcontent.com/pod-product-compliance
Lightning Source LLC
LaVergne TN
LVHW011133210225
804186LV00003B/780

* 9 7 8 1 9 6 0 5 9 6 1 9 2 *